TURNING CRISIS INTO CLARITY

HOW TO SURVIVE OR THRIVE IN THE MIDST OF UNCERTAINTY

Dr. Patrice Berry

Turning Crisis Into Clarity: How to survive or thrive in the midst of uncertainty
Copyright © 2021 by Patrice Berry
Published by LEGACY: U R Legacy Conglomerate
Fredericksburg, VA

ISBN: 978-1-949840-02-5
Printed in the United States of America
© 2021 by Mind Your Legacy, LLC

DISCLAIMER: This book is intended for general information only and is NOT a replacement for diagnosis or treatment by a licensed provider. This publication is meant as a source of valuable information for the reader; however, it is not meant as a substitute for direct expert assistance. If such a level of assistance is required, the services of a competent professional should be sought.

All rights reserved. No part of this book may be reproduced, stored in a retrieval system, or transmitted in any form or by any unauthorized means transmitted in any form or by any means, electronic or mechanical-including photocopying, recording, or by any information storage and retrieval system without permission in writing from the publisher. For direct requests, please email drpatriceberry@gmail.com.

Printed in the United States of America

Dedication

This book is dedicated to all the nurses, doctors, therapists, psychologists, teachers, daycare workers, janitors, grocery store workers, delivery/bus drivers, restaurant employees, and all the other essential workers that helped us get through 2020! May our eyes forever be opened to how overlooked and undervalued some people are within our society. My experiences and the experiences of others that were shared on Clubhouse, Tiktok, Instagram, Facebook, and YouTube helped open the door for this book and so many other opportunities in the midst of tremendous loss and pain. During this time, we learned how to come together, focus on what is really important, and value the people who are truly "essential". I hope that these lessons stick, and that real change will happen to make a better future for generations to come.

CONTENTS

Acknowledgments v
Foreword vi
Content Warning vii
Introduction viii

PART ONE: Survival

Chapter 1: Finding Peace in The Storm 2
Chapter 2: Healing Old Wounds 8
Chapter 3: Surviving Uncertainty 23
Chapter 4: Turning Pain into Purpose 37
Chapter 5: Avoiding Self Sabotage & Impostor Syndrome..... 47
Chapter 6: Helpers Need Help Too 62

PART TWO: Thrive

Chapter 7: Strategies to Build Resilience and Thrive 71
Chapter 8: Holistic Wellness 77
Chapter 9: Coping with Grief & Loss 84
Chapter 10: Forgiveness 94
Chapter 11: Raising Resilient Children 103
Chapter 12: Additional Resources 119
About the Author *135*

Acknowledgements

To my amazing husband, LaMar, thank you for your love and support. You are truly my life partner and I appreciate who you are and all that you do for our family! To our son, thank you for putting mommy's phone in timeout when I was too focused on work or social media! I love you so much and you are our legacy!

To my mom, accountant, friend, and unofficial business coach. Thank you for all your support and for pushing me to be better. To my dad, thank you for being one of my biggest supporters and for encouraging me. To my brothers and my sister, I love you all beyond words!

To my friends, thank you for your love and support! I look forward to face-to-face meetings again! To my Tiktok community, I am so thankful for each and every one of you! Thank you for supporting me and my content! Tiktok is now one of my favorite social media apps and you all make my day a little brighter and help remind me why I started creating content! This has been an amazing journey and I cannot wait for all that will continue to come!

Foreword

This is one of my greatest honors. You see, I have known the author before her birth. I am her mom who happens to also be an entrepreneur, motivational speaker, and international bestselling author. This book didn't start with these pages, it started the moment she was born. For many of you, the crisis was the mechanism that got you to this spot in time, but it is not where you began.

Tucked within these pages you can gain insight, bravery, healing, and awareness. Be open to the tools and revelation so that you can pivot from where you are right now in life to be greater. This quote by Dr. Berry states it best: "Often we FIGHT the PRESENT, RUN from the PAST, and WORRY about the FUTURE".

This amazing heartfelt resource guide can help each of us to manage uncertainty better. Now is the time to impact your present, heal from your past, and empower you to visualize your better future. Whether your immediate need is to survive what you've been through, or to thrive, this is a must-read. Crisis will come and go; however, how we go through it and move forward is priceless. Finally, I will end with this Napoleon Hill quote, "Within every adversity, every failure, every heartache carries with it the seed of an equivalent or a greater benefit."

Johnnie Lloyd

Content/Trigger Warning

THIS BOOK CONTAINS EDUCATIONAL INFORMATION AND REFERENCES TO THE FOLLOWING:

- Trauma including:
  - Childhood trauma
  - Emotional abuse
  - Sexual abuse
  - Physical abuse
  - Neglect
  - Domestic violence
  - Spiritual Abuse
  - Natural Disasters
  - Compassion fatigue/secondary trauma
  - Miscarriage/loss of a child
  - Community violence
  - Pandemic-COVID-19
- Substance abuse
- Suicide
- Self-Injury
- Grief

DISCLAIMER: This book is intended for general information only and is NOT a replacement for diagnosis or treatment by a licensed provider. This publication is meant as a source of valuable information for the reader; however, it is not meant as a substitute for direct expert assistance. If such a level of assistance is required, the services of a competent professional should be sought. Chapter 12 has resources about how to find a therapist.

CRISIS INFO: If you are in crisis, please call the National Suicide Hotline at 1-800-273-8255 or text HOME to 741741. For international hotlines or emergency numbers check out https://findahelpline.com

Introduction

The inspiration for this book came during one of the most painful and joyous times of my life. The saying, "you write what you know" is so true. I never imagined that my first book would be about surviving and thriving during one of the most turbulent, joyous, and chaotic years of my life, but here we are! In 2020, I actively practiced all of the skills I teach my clients and monitored my own wellbeing in the midst of a global pandemic, racial unrest, and social/political strife. As a licensed psychologist with over fifteen years of clinical experience teaching clients how to manage their emotions and behavior, I started my career working with children and teens that often struggled with accepting "no" as an answer, delaying gratification, and tolerating basic changes in their everyday life. There are so many ways in which life prepared me for this moment, and I will share some of those stories with you along with specific skills, resources, and tools to survive and/or thrive when you face a crisis.

If you google the word "survive" you will find many definitions. The one that will be used for this book is "continue to live or exist, especially in spite of danger or hardship" (definition of survive - Google Search, 2011). Throughout this book, we will examine how our brains are wired for survival, and how, sometimes, our first instinct is not always healthy. The first section is all about survival, and every chapter incorporates additional resources and tools to help you along your journey. Section one lays the foundation for the tools to develop resilience and thrive in section two. Here is my favorite definition of the word thrive as it relates to this book, to "grow or develop well or vigorously" (definition of thrive - Google Search, 2018).

Finally, this book ends with a plethora of great resources separated by topic in Chapter 12: Additional Resources. Please do not wait until the end if you are presently in need of specific tools or support as you journey through this book. It is my heartfelt desire that individuals who are initially hesitant to seek out therapy/treatment, will find the right individual to support them towards their goals as necessary. My first therapist was not the right fit for me and led me to think that there was something wrong with therapy as a practice. The truth was the first individual was the wrong fit. Eventually, the third therapist I engaged with was the right fit for me and helped me on my own healing journey. Here is a list of the information included in Chapter 12:

- How to find a therapist, red and green flags in therapy, and how to address conflict/questions with your therapist

- Therapy versus coaching

- Psychologist, Psychiatrist, Social Worker, Counselor...what is the difference?

- Therapeutic approaches and treatment modalities

- Resources: trauma, parenting, emotion regulation/self-help, & Dialectical Behavior Therapy (DBT)

- Additional resources to check out on YouTube, Tik Tok, & Podcasts

My personal style is to provide you with way more recommendations than needed so that you have options to tailor your process to the best fit for you. You can look up the books that are recommended for additional reading and see what interests you. It is also my goal that the resource pages be used later as things arise down the road. You will learn in these pages, one of the best ways we can address uncertainty and anxiety is to expect it to show up.

To give up the notion that life is full of predictability and certainty. Instead, let's prepare for the unknown and remember the ways we have successfully navigated difficult situations in the past.

REFERENCES

definition of survive - Google Search. (2011). Google.com.

definition of thrive - Google Search. (2018). Google.com.

PART 1
SURVIVAL

Chapter 1

FINDING PEACE IN THE STORM

Have you ever been caught in a downpour on your way home that was so heavy you could barely see what was right in front of you? The sky gets dark, the rain pours down, and even though you know exactly how to get home, you snap into a heightened sense of your surroundings. Normally in those situations I reduce my speed, turn down the volume of my music, focus on what I can see, monitor my breath and emotions, and keep my eyes on the other drivers around me. Many of these same strategies can help us in the storms of life.

In the midst of chaos, we often default to survival mode, so it can be helpful to prepare for difficulties as you see them approaching. My preparation for the changes that would impact me professionally due to COVID-19 began in August 2019 when I had to lay off staff for the first time. I worked for an agency as the director of a school-based counseling program and significant Medicaid changes resulted in the need to cut back staff. We did our best to support staff and help them either transfer to other areas in the company or secure new employment if they wanted to remain within the school system. At that moment, I began to think about my options if that job was no longer available. My salaried position provided safety and security and I doubt that I would have started my own private practice if my position did not come to an end in late March of 2020.

In order to find peace in the storm, we first have to acknowledge that we are, in fact, in a storm. There are people that try to go through life being overly positive and not admit when they struggle (toxic positivity). In the past, we may have viewed this as a strength. Now, because of the work of Brené Brown and others, we know that true strength lies in being vulnerable and being able to ask for help. We also have to be able to experience our feelings, allowing ourselves to feel within safe and supportive environments. We often add judgments or assign value to emotions, when instead we should view each one as an opportunity to experience our humanity and learn more about ourselves and others. We will always have emotions that we prefer, but there is nothing wrong with feeling angry, sad, frustrated, guilty, etc.

Avoiding or canceling emotions is not a long-term strategy and doing so can lead to a variety of physical and psychological concerns down the road. You eventually have to deal with the emotion in order to heal. Instead of avoiding the storm, let's learn how to safely navigate it. Each person will individualize how they do this and what works best for them according to their past, current situation and resources, and desired future. Healing can only take place where safety is felt. A person can physically and emotionally be safe, yet not feel safe. The coming chapters will discuss how our brains are wired for survival and constantly scanning for threats or danger. We can learn how to use times of safety and comfort to help us prepare for more difficult times in the future.

In January of 2020, I began to build my brand on social media and started the process of setting up a legal business. My plan was to launch in August of 2020; however, circumstances pushed that date up significantly. I also did not plan to do telehealth (online counseling). Prior to COVID, I preferred in-person counseling and now I love the flexibility that telehealth provides my clients. Due to being connected with other counselors in my community, I was also able to hear about and attend a free 18-hour telehealth training to further prepare me for this new venture. My student loans being on hold during this time also helped free me financially to leave the agency's salaried position and launch my own business. I viewed walking away from an agency that I loved in 2020 as an opportunity to step into my purpose. I also did not realize the happiness and freedom that I would feel working on my own terms. Still, there are times that I miss my former coworkers and the certainty and resources that come with working for a larger agency. Yet, I know that leaving was one of the best decisions of my life and it was because of the COVID-19 pandemic. We can learn a lot about ourselves and others in the midst of uncertainty. A crisis can either trigger chaos or you can turn the crisis into clarity based on how you do the following:

1. Perceive and adapt to events
2. Manage available resources
3. Embrace the ability to ask for help and support when needed
4. Connect with your community
5. Focus on what is in your control and prioritize what is urgent and important
6. Let go of the things that are out of your control and find felt safety

Flexibility is key to navigating the storm with a peaceful mind and body. Dr. Carol Dweck (2008) coined the term "growth mindset" and contrasted having a "fixed mindset". A growth or flexible mindset is a belief that effort contributes to success more than innate abilities. It is a growth mindset that is willing to make mistakes and try to do hard things. With a flexible mindset, failure is viewed as a learning opportunity. People with a fixed or rigid mindset are more likely to give up when things get hard and struggle to believe there is anything they can do to change their situation. The chart below gives some examples of the difference between a fixed and growth mindset.

Fixed Mindset Examples: Rigid & Limiting	**Growth Mindset Examples:** Flexible and Freeing
Failure was due to a lack of ability	Failure is an opportunity to learn, grown, and try again
Difficult problems can't be solved	Difficult problems can be solved with effort and support
Focus is on what I don't have and can't do	Focus is on what I do have and can do
Things should stay the same	Things always evolve and change
It needs to be completed and my way is the only way	It needs to be completed and there are multiple ways to solve this problem

Research has shown that people and animals experience learned helplessness if they do not get relief from their pain. It can trigger the belief that nothing matters or will change this situation and to just give up. Learned helplessness can also be seen in children. One study identified the following characteristics of learned helplessness in children who struggled with reading (Butkowsky, & Willows 1980): failure to ask for help, giving up on the task, low frustration tolerance, lack of effort, low self-esteem, lack of motivation, procrastination, and passivity.

Often people make judgments about a person's life or their willingness to "do better" without fully understanding their story. It is my objective that the information in this book will validate the experiences of people who are struggling and help them to understand the roots of problematic thinking and behaviors. If you begin to feel judged, please stop, take a breath, and give yourself some compassion. This statement has helped me in my own life "people do the best they can with what they have". The problem is when their best is causing problems and they do not work on changing it. I also try to be vulnerable and share times that I have struggled with many of the concepts listed in this book. One of my favorite sayings on social media is to not compare your real life to other people's highlights.

In order to find peace in the storm, you need to prepare, be flexible, be connected to others, acknowledge the storm, let go of judgments of ourselves and others, accept and adjust to the new normal, monitor your health (physical, emotional, spiritual), and practice mindfulness and gratitude. It is also very important to not compare your response to others in the same storm. Some people will speed right through the storm as though nothing is happening. This may be dangerous for them and comparing yourself to them will only make you focus on what you are not. Instead, continue to make progress at your pace and safely work through your storm. In the next chapter, we will examine how a crisis can trigger old wounds.

RESOURCES

- *Emotional Intelligence: Why It Can Matter More Than IQ* by Daniel Goleman
- *Mindset: The New Psychology of Success* by Carol S. Dweck

REFERENCES

Butkowsky, I. S., & Willows, D. M. (1980). Cognitive-motivational characteristics of children varying in reading ability: Evidence for learned helplessness in poor readers. *Journal of Educational Psychology, 72*(3), 408–422.

Center for Substance Abuse Treatment (US. 2014). *Understanding the Impact of Trauma*. Nih.gov; Substance Abuse and Mental Health Services Administration (US).
https://www.ncbi.nlm.nih.gov/books/NBK207191

Dweck, C. S. (2008). *Mindset.* Ballantine Books.

Goleman, D. (1995). *Emotional intelligence: Why it can matter more than IQ.* New York: Bantam Books.

CHAPTER 2

HEALING OLD WOUNDS

The word trauma comes from the Greek word meaning "wound" and can refer to both physical and psychological injuries (*Dictionary*, 2021). A crisis has a way of exposing unhealed wounds and/or reopening old wounds. It is important to remember that pain has a purpose. It lets us know that something is not right and/or needs our attention. There are times when pain is chronic, and we become numb to the pain. This is often a way to cope with chronic distress. Here are some signs that you may be walking around wounded: unexplained agitation, increased moodiness/emotional reactivity, avoiding people and situations that remind you of an old wound (unless doing this for safety reasons), increasing feelings of guilt and shame, low self-esteem, difficulty thinking about or imagining the future, withdrawing from others, and feeling disconnected or not feeling anything at all.

If you have ever been to therapy, during the first appointment you are asked a variation of this question: "So tell me about your childhood". Looking at the past can help us understand the present. When someone describes having a chaotic and unstable childhood, that information helps me locate the root of their difficulty with change and rigid thinking. Past wounds do not excuse someone's behavior. Instead, it helps me better understand their struggle and identify skills deficits. The past does not define the future, yet it does impact how a person may perceive and/or respond to a situation.

Trauma is defined as anything that is "too much, too fast, too soon - and there is not enough time to integrate the experience"

(What is Trauma? — BodyWise Foundation, 2014). Just because someone goes through a negative life event, that does not mean that they will develop trauma symptoms. This is why I talk about the importance of building resilience in children in Chapter 11, so that we can better prepare them for uncertainty and challenges in the future. As a parent, I never want anything bad to happen to my child and it is my mission to keep him safe. However, we live in an unpredictable world, and I want my child to be prepared for whatever life may throw at him. This does not ensure that he will never need therapy or support. I view seeking therapy and seeking support as a normal part of life, just like going to the medical doctor for an annual checkup or taking my car for routine maintenance.

Adverse Childhood Experiences Study (ACEs)

One of the most important studies in recent years is the Adverse Childhood Experiences Study. The Adverse Childhood Experiences questionnaire contains ten questions that ask about negative experiences in childhood. The questionnaire can be found on multiple sites online including www.acestoohigh.com. According to the CDC, "ACEs are common. About 61% of adults surveyed across 25 states reported that they had experienced at least one type of ACE, and nearly 1 in 6 reported they had experienced four or more types of ACEs." (*Adverse Childhood Experiences (ACEs)*, 2021). Based on research completed by the CDC and others, ACEs contribute to many negative social, emotional, and health outcomes. The higher the number of ACEs, the greater the risk for chronic physical/medical problems, emotional and/or behavioral issues, and problems within relationships. (*Adverse Childhood Experiences (ACEs*, 2021). I include this questionnaire in my new client paperwork to screen for childhood trauma.

It is important to note that two people can go through the same experience and have drastically different perceptions and responses. This is why I switched from asking people if they experienced trauma in childhood and instead provide the ACEs questionnaire and inquire about significant negative life events. There are extended versions of this questionnaire that also ask about exposure to community violence and experiences of racism. Our brains are wired to survive, to see the bad and overlook the good. When you are in survival brain, you do not need to focus on the positive and instead need to focus on the negative to survive. The problem with this thinking is that it can be activated in neutral or even positive situations. We may misperceive an event as threatening that is safe. Early experiences can also influence this, including the messages we received as young kids about what is safe and unsafe.

Trauma and the Brain

Understanding what happens in a brain that has experienced trauma and/or been exposed to multiple negative life events, often helps validate my clients' experience. I have been doing this work for a while, so I frequently ask about the thoughts and experiences that would be considered "odd" if the person had not experienced trauma. In light of their history, I understand and validate their experience. Please remember that validation is not approval. I can validate the experience of being easily triggered while processing the negative impact it is having on the person's relationships. There are resources linked at the end of this chapter and in Chapter 12 that provide more information on this topic if you find this helpful. Once I finish writing this book, I'm excited to listen to Oprah Winfrey and Dr. Bruce Perry's book "What Happened to You".

In previous books and published articles, Dr. Bruce Perry has discussed his NeuroSequential Model of Therapeutics. Those are a lot of big words to describe that the brain develops from the "bottom-up" and must be healed in that order as well. Often we try to rationalize our trauma and think our way out of it, and if the trauma occurred in the brain stem, those primitive areas of the brain must be healed first. Later I will talk more about adoption, but this work has transformed my work with children who have experienced trauma. Parents often complained to me that their 12-year-old child would revert to behaviors that were more common of a 3 or 4-year-old and that was a sign that they were regressing to the age of their "wound". The amygdala and more primitive and emotional areas of the brain do not respond to language and are often triggered by it. Instead, it often responds to sensory input like movement (rocking, walking), light pressure (weighted blanket), sour or hot candy, hugs (if requested/accepted), and/or something soft like a stuffed animal or blanket. There have also been times when I met individuals who were so busy surviving their chaotic childhoods that they never learned appropriate social skills, emotion regulation, or how to resolve conflict.

To simplify things, we have a thinking brain and an emotional brain. The thinking brain is our neocortex, our more advanced thinking and problem-solving. While our emotional brain is the brainstem and limbic system. The emotional brain typically kicks into gear when we are in a very stressful or dangerous situation. When the amygdala senses threat, it sets off an alarm. The thinking brain quickly assesses the situation and goes "offline", and the emotional brain activates and triggers our survival responses. Then when things calm down and return to normal, the thinking brain comes back online, and we can think about and process the experience. The hippocampus stores our most recent conscious memories, for example, what I ate for dinner in an ordered and sequential way. Whereas trauma memories end up scattered as these mental fragments throughout our brain that can "pop up" at unexpected times. When we sense danger, the only goal is to survive and get through the experience. The following chart has example trauma responses.

Fight	*Arguing *Aggression (physical, verbal, emotional)
Flight	*Avoiding conflict/situations/or people *Leaving or feeling intense urge to leave situations
Freeze	*Dissociation/disconnecting *Emotionally numb *Indecisive
Fawn	*People pleasing; overworking *Difficulty making decisions due to fear of letting people down *Perfectionism *Avoiding conflict *Over-apologizing

For some individuals that have experienced childhood trauma, adoption, racial and/or intergenerational trauma, and/or combat trauma, their amygdala stops functioning properly and constantly "sounds the alarm". This makes a person perceive threat or danger in every situation including positive and neutral situations. It can also be difficult because logically they often know that there is no real danger. Sometimes this is also referred to as a survival loop where their trauma responses are continually being triggered. Dr. Eric Gentry's work helped me gain new tools to address this with clients. During a training for mental health professionals, he asked, "How many of you are 100% safe right now?". I did not raise my hand because I felt 90-98% safe but I could not say that I was 100% safe. In a room full of about 50 people only one person raised their hand and to this day I am convinced that they had attended one of his training sessions in the past. Dr. Gentry went on to explain that we were perceiving a threat based on our own past negative experiences. When there was no active threat, the goal should be to feel 100% safe. People would argue with him saying, "what if event

X happens?" and he would clarify that there was no evidence of danger, only hypothetical situations.

There is a difference between being vigilant and being hypervigilant. Hypervigilance puts us on guard all the time and does not allow the person to enjoy peaceful and safe moments. When someone is in "survival brain" all of the time, they may misinterpret neutral and positive situations as negative. For example, someone who meets a nice new person may say, "there is just something about them that I don't like, I just can't put my finger on it". When abuse and trauma are the norm, safety can feel unsafe. This behavior likely helped survive unsafe situations and becomes problematic when those same survival tactics are used in safe situations.

Amygdala Hijack

Daniel Goleman coined the term "amygdala hijack" *(Goleman, D. 1995)*, where the amygdala during times of perceived threat hijacks the thinking brain and activates our autonomic nervous system. This part of our brain increases our heart rate, narrows our vision, empties our bladder and bowels, releases cortisol and adrenaline, increases sweat and/or chills, and causes our breathing to become short and shallow. In a situation where a bear is chasing me, this would be perfect because all of those physiological responses would increase my chances of survival. However, this response can be triggered by seemingly benign situations like hearing the word "no", perceived rejection, or a change in plans. The goal is to get back to our sympathetic nervous system as quickly as possible if our stress response is triggered and there is no danger. To re-engage your sympathetic nervous system and get out of survival brain, you can try one of the following (find the technique that works best for you):

- Grounding techniques (5 things you can see, 4 things you can touch, 3 things you can hear, 2 things you can smell, and 1 thing you can taste)
- Physical activity/exercise
- Meditation/mindfulness/prayer
- Deep breathing
- Playing with animals
- Splash cold water on our face or ice on the back of the neck

There are ways we can prepare for situations that are stressful like practicing the techniques listed above regularly so that they can become a habit.

Let's Talk About "Triggers"

The word "trigger" is overused right now, so let's clarify some things. For people who have a history of experiencing trauma, certain situations, people, or places may trigger their painful past. This is often described as a trauma trigger. There is a big difference between someone not liking something and a trauma trigger. Negative emotions can be triggered; however, overuse of this word can minimize and invalidate the experience of people who have experienced real trauma or are in recovery. It is also important to distinguish between a trauma trigger and a flashback. Flashbacks can be triggered but every trigger is not a flashback. The main difference between the two is that a flashback involves re-experiencing/reliving the past event as though it was happening now, and a trauma trigger reminds you of the event. A trigger may bring up some emotional and/or physiological symptoms without a mental return to the past event. Some alternatives provided on a recent Tik Tok video by some of my followers are activated, unsettled, rattled, or uncomfortable.

Also, did you know that there is no such thing as a "bad" emotion? Now there are such things as negative behaviors and inappropriate expression of emotion. Behaviors are separate from emotion and adults and children should be permitted to feel. Often in our society, we only let males express anger and happiness and they are denied the full expression of emotion in attempts to not appear "weak". Expressing emotion appropriately is not weak. When we let our emotions out in healthy ways, they typically will not spill out in unhealthy and explosive ways. Also, if someone has grown up with a caregiver that did not express any emotion or expressed their emotions in very exaggerated ways, the child may struggle to appropriately express their own emotions. Uncontrolled expressions of emotion are also problematic and quite often not even representative of the specific emotions being felt. This is where learning strategies that help you remain or become calm and find appropriate outlets for your emotions can be helpful.

Veterans/Active-Duty Military

My dad is retired military and I have multiple family members that currently serve and have served in the military. Many of my clients are veterans or active military. Some people join the military to escape negative home lives and they may continue to experience trauma symptoms related to their childhood. Some individuals experience combat stress/trauma and develop Post-Traumatic Stress Disorder (PTSD), Traumatic Brain Injuries, and/or other symptoms of traumatic stress. Military experience can harden some people to day-to-day life as a civilian and they may struggle to "turn off" the part of their brains that had to be on 24/7 to survive warzones and/or combat situations. There are individuals whose combat stress symptoms do not emerge until they return home due to their behavior in combat. Here are some signs of Combat Stress from an article on Military One Source (2020):

- Irritability and anger outbursts
- Excessive fear and worry
- Headaches and fatigue
- Depression and apathy
- Loss of appetite
- Problems sleeping
- Changes in behavior or personality

There are a lot of great trauma treatments that are effective. Acknowledging that there is an issue and seeking help are the first steps on the road to recovery. As a side note, try to find a therapist that understands military service will support and validate your experience, and will not be put off by the stories you may have.

Racial Trauma/Intergenerational Trauma

Research on intergenerational trauma began with studies on Holocaust survivors and continued looking at the impact of slavery on African Americans. Racial trauma is real and in 2020 with the murders of George Floyd, Breonna Taylor, and Ahmad Ahmaud Arbery in the midst of everyone being on hyper-alert due to COVID-19, the world was able to see what many Black people in America have known for generations.

To break the cycles of abuse and trauma we need to acknowledge the hurt and the pain, fight for equity, and learn new strategies (e.g., new parenting techniques) to help make a better world for future generations. The symptoms of racial trauma are very similar to the symptoms of PTSD. When racial trauma is triggered, please take care of yourself and give yourself space to step away from watching the news or the video of an incident. If you need to seek therapy, find a culturally aware therapist and ask about their approach to the subject of racial trauma. Please also know that intergenerational healing is real too. We can heal and pass those healthy coping mechanisms on to the next generation as well.

Adoption

Throughout my career, I have worked with many individuals impacted by the foster care system and adoption. While there are a lot of positive aspects of adoption, in this section, I'm going to focus on the following seven core issues related to adoption: loss, rejection, guilt/shame, grief, identity, intimacy, and master and control (Silverstein & Kaplan, 1982). Adoptees, birth families, and adoptive families (including birth children) can experience these seven things. Many of the families I have worked with also described experiencing "ambiguous loss" (a term coined by Dr. Pauline Boss)—unanswered questions and a lack of closure. There are a lot of myths about adoption, and I think it is important that we dispel these immediately. The impact of adoption for the birth family, adoptive family, and adoptee are lifelong.

Here are some common myths, truths, and general tips related to adoption:

1. MYTH: Adopting a baby or younger child will lessen the behavior problems because they grew up in your home. **TRUTH:** There are a lot of factors that go into this, and individuals adopted as infants or young children still feel the grief, loss, and trauma, related to adoption. An older child may have received the appropriate prenatal care, emotional, and social support that places them at an advantage compared to a toddler that experienced significant neglect and abuse. **TIPS:** All children test boundaries, make mistakes, and need to learn how to manage their emotions and behaviors. In my experience, children who have been adopted often struggle with lying, stealing, hoarding, etc., and may need help and support to address these behaviors. If you see behavior issues that are outside of the norm, seek support from an adoption-informed counselor and doctor for tips and recommendations. Seek support within other adoption support groups.

2. MYTH: Adopting a child will fill the empty void within my life. **TRUTH:** A child is not responsible for filling/fulfilling adults. **TIPS:** Adoption is plan B for some individuals following infertility and/or child loss. Please address these wounds before adopting a child. No child can ever fill that space. If adoption is your plan A, go in with realistic expectations.

3. MYTH: It is best for the child to be cut off from their birth family and connections to adjust to their adoptive family. **TRUTH:** Research has shown that safe contact with the birth family is recommended if possible. If that is not possible, supporting your child in finding their birth family in the future, can often help deepen their relationship with you as they try to get important questions answered. **TIPS:** Partner with an adoption competent therapist if you are having difficulty knowing what information to share with your child and what information to withhold. You never want to speak negatively about the birth family.

4. MYTH: Adoptive children should "act" like they want to be adopted. **TRUTH:** Adoptive parents should never place the child's behavior as a prerequisite for adoption. Children do the best they can and ultimatums like "act like you want to be a part of this family" often increase negative behaviors due to triggering attachment trauma. **TIPS:** Be a safe space for your child and address any behavioral triggers you (adoptive parent) have with a therapist before adoption. Often the behaviors that trigger the adult are related to their unhealed wounds. If a child is being aggressive or engaging in inappropriate behavior, seek appropriate treatment and establish safety.

5. MYTH: They are my child, and I should be able to discipline them however I please (related to using physical discipline and authoritarian parenting). **TRUTH:** This is especially problematic and common within religious communities. All adoption involves attachment wounds and trauma. Physical discipline and rigid parenting inflict additional wounds and damage the relationship. **TIPS:** Learn and implement strategies like Trust-Based Relational Intervention (TBRI) where you CONNECT before you CORRECT.

6. MYTH: If my child loves me, they will not think about or ask about their birth family. Why isn't my love enough? **TRUTH:** Every child will wonder about their birth family, and this should be encouraged and normalized. Stay away from words like "real" parents. Your child will wonder about their identity, who they look like, and where they come from. **TIPS:** If possible, maintain a relationship with the birth family (if safe for the child) and manage your own emotions about seeing the child with their birth family. It can often bring up significant feelings of grief, loss, and identity within the adoptive parents. Address this with your supportive community.

7. MYTH: My adopted child has been in my home for a year and should be adjusted by now. **TRUTH:** Your adopted child will be impacted by adoption for the rest of their life. There will be critical times, especially around transitions that behavior and/or emotional issues are very common. **TIPS:** Adoption has a lifelong impact and I have worked with adult adoptees that continue to need therapeutic support to address issues related to grief and loss, emotion regulation, self-esteem, etc. There is nothing wrong with needing additional help and support.

8. MYTH: Race/ethnic identity does not matter; we are raising our child to not see color. **TRUTH:** Race/ethnic identity is a part of your child's culture and denying them access to this part of them can cause significant problems down the road. **TIPS:** Connect your child with their culture and place yourself in situations where you are the minority. Do not let people who are racist or say racist things be around your child (even extended family). Connect your child with members of their racial/ethnic community.

In Trust-Based Relational Intervention (TBRI) they discuss the importance of felt safety (Purvis et al., 2013). Often the adoptive families that I work with describe their home as safe physically and emotionally; however, their child may not experience it as safe. There are simple things that adoptive parents can do like avoiding needless power struggles, finding ways to share control with their child, finding ways to say yes (For example, a child asks for an apple right before dinner and the parent says," yes you can have it after you eat your dinner"), creating structure and routine (not rigid), using attachment informed parenting, and the parents managing their emotions when triggered. Also, remember that progress is not linear, and you may take one step forward and two steps back.

Conclusion

The past does not determine your future and you are more than just the sum of your experience. The healing process can be messy, and things may feel a little worse before they feel better. It is very similar to working out for the first time after not being active for a while, your body will feel sore at first, and then it will adjust. We can all learn how to navigate through a crisis and increase our tolerance for uncertainty. The storm may trigger your stress response, and there are things you can do to keep moving forward. I hope this is empowering and remember that some moments will be easier to manage than others. Uncertainty can open the door to confusion and chaos, my ambition is that you remember how to get back to clarity, safety, and peace.

RESOURCES

- *The Deepest Well: Healing the Long-Term Effects of Childhood Adversity* by Burke Harris M.D., Nadine
- *The Body Keeps the Score: Brain, Mind, and Body in the Healing of Trauma Hardcover* – by Bessel van der Kolk M.D.
- *Complex PTSD Workbook: A Mind-Body Approach to Regaining Emotional Control and Becoming Whole* by Arielle Schwartz
- *The Wounds Within: A Veteran, a PTSD Therapist, and a Nation Unprepared* by Mark I. Nickerson
- *Post Traumatic Slave Syndrome, Revised Edition: : America's Legacy of Enduring Injury and Healing* by Joy a Degruy
- *The Unapologetic Guide to Black Mental Health: Navigate an Unequal System, Learn Tools for Emotional Wellness, and Get the Help you Deserve* by Rheeda Walker PhD , Na'im Akbar PhD (Foreword)
- *White Fragility: Why It's So Hard for White People to Talk About Racism* by Robin DiAngelo
- *How to Be an Antiracist* by Ibram X. Kendi
- *Seven Core Issues in Adoption and Permanency: A Comprehensive Guide to Promoting Understanding and Healing In Adoption, Foster Care, Kinship Families and Third Party Reproduction* by Sharon Roszia, Allison Davis Maxon
- *Why is Dad So Mad?* by Seth Kastle
- *Why is Mom So Mad?: A Book About PTSD and Military Families* by Seth Kastle
- www.ambiguousloss.com
- www.adoptionsupport.org

REFERENCES

Adverse Childhood Experiences (ACEs). (2021).
https://www.cdc.gov/violenceprevention/aces/index.html

Combat Stress and PTSD Symptoms and Recovery | Military OneSource. (2020, December 2). Military OneSource. https://www.militaryonesource.mil/health-wellness/wounded-warriors/ptsd-and-traumatic-brain-injury/understanding-and-dealing-with-combat-stress-and-ptsd/

Dictionary. (2021). Www.dictionary.com.
https://www.dictionary.com/browse/trauma

Goleman, D. (1995). *Emotional intelligence: Why it can matter more than IQ.* New York: Bantam Books.

Purvis, K. B., Cross, D. R., Dansereau, D. F., & Parris, S. R. (2013). Trust-Based Relational Intervention (TBRI): A Systemic Approach to Complex Developmental Trauma. Child & youth services, 34(4), 360–386. https://doi.org/10.1080/0145935X.2013.859906

Silverstein, D. N., & Kaplan, S. (1982). *Seven core issues in adoption.*

What ACEs/PCEs do you have? (2011, November 18). ACEs Too High; ACEs Too High. https://acestoohigh.com/got-your-ace-score/

What Are ACEs? And How Do They Relate to Toxic Stress? (2020, October 30). Center on the Developing Child at Harvard University. https://developingchild.harvard.edu/resources/aces-and-toxic-stress-frequently-asked-questions/

What is Trauma? — BodyWise Foundation. (2014). *RISE UP.* RISE UP. https://www.bodywisefoundation.org/what-is-trauma

CHAPTER 3

SURVIVING UNCERTAINTY

"Don't fight uncertainty. The more you fight it, the more pain you will experience. Accept what you can and cannot control." —Dr. Patrice Berry

One of the most difficult aspects of a crisis is uncertainty. More often than not, you do not know how long it will last or the impact it will have. This triggers a variety of emotions including anxiety, worry, frustration, anger, and/or fear. To stay grounded we often have to take a step back, consider our resources, and see what is within our control.

Focus

One of the most important things to do in the midst of a crisis is to focus. The crisis can be distracting, so identifying and focusing on your priorities is key. The chaos around you will stand out and you will have to look for solutions to your problems. The problems often yell while the solutions whisper. It is also important to expect uncertainty and prepare for any obstacles that may come. In 2020, my husband and I had a discussion about how we would handle it if our son's daycare closed, so we were already prepared when we received the email that our son's class was closed for two weeks. You will not be able to prepare for every scenario and yet it is important to solve your problems with your thinking brain and not your survival brain. Survival brain will tell you to buy up all the toilet tissue, purchase all the canned goods (even ones that you know no one in your family will ever eat), and sit in line for hours to get gas every day (even though your tank is full). It is important to respond to the crisis and not react out of emotion. **If you or your child is having difficulties be sure to check the common acronym HALT. Are you (or they) hungry, angry, lonely, or tired?** If yes, address the need and then check in with how you are feeling.

Give your attention to what you CAN control and LET GO of what you cannot. Uncertainty breeds questions that are often out of your control. When will schools reopen? When will things be back to normal? How long will we have to wear masks? Will we need regular shots of the COVID vaccine? Will COVID ever go away? None of us know the definite answers to these questions and focusing on questions with no solutions feeds anxiety.

Did you know that anxiety and worry are actually good things? A little anxiety can motivate a student to prepare for a test, while too much anxiety makes their mind go blank when they take the test. A little worry helps you to problem-solve difficult tasks and yet too much worry makes it difficult to make any decision or think at all. The work of Lynn Lyons and Reid Wilson in the book *Anxious Kids, Anxious Parents* helped me to change my approach when clients present with anxiety. Anxiety activates our survival brain and the major message in the previously mentioned book is that anxiety wants certainty and control. Those are two things that you do not have during a crisis.

Gratitude

Our brains are wired for survival, so we have to intentionally look for the good. This is where adding a practice of gratitude to your life may be helpful. This is a simple activity that I recommended to individuals, families, and workplaces. The directions are to take a small piece of paper and write down something that you are grateful for every day and then at the end of the week or month going through it. If you feel like there is a lot of complaining and negativity in your environment, going through the jar weekly may be more helpful. There are so many things that can go wrong in the midst of a crisis and there are also some things that are ok. Notice I did not say perfect, what we want, or what we were expecting. I did not expect to walk away from a salaried position in March of 2020 and yet it was one of the best decisions of my life. We can be grateful for things we do not like. For example, I do not like wearing a mask and I am grateful that I was sick a lot less due to wearing it. I also say to start a practice of gratitude because it may not come naturally. After about 30 days of engaging in this practice, many people report feeling less anxious, less depressed, and more hopeful about the future. They also report appreciating what they have even more. It is inevitable that there will be losses in a crisis, but it will also produce some gains. I'm grateful that we were able to spend more time together and there was less pressure to socialize with others. This extra time allowed me to launch two businesses within a year. I am also grateful that I have the support and love of my family. Nothing is perfect, and I am grateful for what I have.

Social media can sometimes have you consciously or subconsciously comparing your life to others. Be mindful of how your time online impacts your thoughts and feelings about what you have. Please do not compare your real life to the highlights other people choose to share. If you look at my social media, I do not post the times I barely made it to work because of traffic, or when I accidentally started my coffee without putting a cup in my single-serve coffee maker, or the times I lose my keys or all the other things that happen in my real life. This may be why I like Tik Tok, because on that platform you see me with no makeup, sometimes with no beauty filter, with my hair in a messy bun, and my daily struggle with avoiding what I do not want to do (mostly my notes and billing). Accepting, appreciating, valuing, and being grateful for my present does not mean that I want to stay in the same place forever. Practicing gratitude does help me enjoy my present and the journey to my destination.

Reframe

Our thinking about a situation can impact how we feel and act. This is why it is important to reframe negative thoughts. The 'safe at home' versus 'stuck at home' was one of my favorite examples of teaching people how to reframe negative thinking. The thought of being stuck at home brings up more feelings of frustration, anger, and anxiety than the thought of being safe at home. There are some common thought traps that we can fall into when stressed, anxious, or depressed. Here are some examples:

Thinking Trap	Reaction	Reframe
All or nothing thinking/Black or white thinking	Things never go my way	Sometimes things do not go my way (learn to accept the gray)
Snowballing	If they do not turn in this assignment homework, then they are going to fail the 9th grade, and then they are never going to college, and then they will live with us forever	Problem-solve your child turning in their assignments and focus on the more immediate consequence (e.g., getting a zero)
Discounting the positive	I received a positive review from work, but it was only because of COVID.	Accept the compliment and address any roots to/reasons for difficulty accepting and seeing the positive.
Catastrophizing	If I am late for work they will fire me, and we will be homeless.	My boss warned me about being late to work, I'm going to get up earlier to make it on time

Be mindful of your self-talk and if it is consistently negative, start reframing how you think about yourself. Often people that have negative self-talk, would say something positive or give good advice to a friend. If this is an issue, try to start talking to yourself as though you are your friend.

Dr. Carol Dweck popularized having a growth mindset in her 2006 book *Mindset: The new psychology of success.* People can either have a fixed or a growth mindset. A fixed mindset is focused on what is not working, what I can't do, and everything I am not in a situation. It is described as being rigid. When someone with a fixed mindset sees a problem as too difficult, they will not even try because they are already defeated in their mind. Someone with a growth mindset sees problems to be solved and believes that effort determines the outcome. They are also open to failing and things not going their way, because they can learn during the process. A growth mindset is described as being flexible. Anyone can shift from being more rigid to being more flexible in their thinking. I will be honest and admit that there are some things that I have a rigid mentality about. For example, I do not want to understand cars and there is no amount of effort or training that will change my mind. Yet, when it comes to psychology, I am very open and flexible to learning new things. I say this to point out that someone can be rigid in one regard and flexible in another. Rigid thinkers also struggle with change and admiring new situations. When situations happen, I often take a step back and attempt to see the whole picture. If I am operating in survival brain, the first step is to calm my emotions and get into the thinking brain. Survival brain is very rigid and only wants to survive. Thinking brain is open to new possibilities and new things. Rigid thinking is very hesitant to try something new and a flexible thinker is open to trying new things. There are tools in resources linked below and YouTube videos online about developing a growth mindset.

Courage

We need to redefine what it means to be strong. A crisis can show you your strength, even if you cried every day, missed the deadline, and your child did not turn in their homework. It takes courage to stay and finish the task. It takes courage to come out of your comfort zone and ask for help. It takes courage to go to therapy or talk with your doctor about medication options. Take things one day, one minute, one second at a time, and just get through each day. I enjoy telling clients that I am proud of them. Proud that they showed up for therapy, proud that they reached back out after discharge when some major issues came back up, and proud that they made a decision that was best for them and their family. As I have mentioned before, anxiety wants certainty and control. That can increase a person's desire to avoid a situation and remain in their comfort zone. It takes courage to not listen to anxiety and manage the discomfort of pushing through an uncertain situation. The aspiration is that enduring a little discomfort now will lead to a better future. As you prepare to step out and be courageous, please know that negative thoughts about your ability to handle it will arise. This is where you practice saying, "I got this!", "I am just going to give it my best.", "Everyone falls down sometimes...", and press towards your desired goal. Instead of fighting uncertainty, we need to increase our ability to tolerate and accept it.

Limit Negativity

It is important to be mindful of who you are around and what you are listening to. It is my recommendation to limit your news intake during a crisis. Our 24-hour news cycle will talk about an issue from 2 days ago as though it is a present and imminent threat. My favorite is when a certain news anchor starts every segment with "breaking news", despite the information presented being the same as the previous host. Be aware of how watching or reading the news impacts you. For me, reading an article is less distressing than watching a video of a crisis or major issue. It is also important to remember that children see and hear everything. So, limiting the news when they are around, even if you think they cannot understand what is going on. Try to be around a few positive people and limit your time around people who drain your energy, and you leave feeling worse.

There is a difference between someone occasionally venting and someone constantly emotionally dumping on you. A person that is venting is often open to changing their behavior and you leave the conversation feeling as though you have supported a friend. Emotional dumping is when a person is unable or unwilling to consider alternatives, feedback, or another perspective. After being emotionally dumped on, a person typically feels heavy and may worry about the other individual. As a friend, you can set boundaries around emotional dumping and encourage your friend to seek help. If they are currently receiving help, encourage them to make sure that they are bringing up those important topics in their sessions. I have found that many people emotionally dump on their friends and then do not open up in therapy.

Creating Safety

In the midst of a crisis, it is important to create felt safety for yourself and your family. First, we start off by making sure that your basic needs are met including food, water, shelter, employment/finances. Then we would want to make sure that educational needs and needs for belonging are met as best we can, managing what is in our control. If those needs are met, practicing mindfulness can be very helpful because anxiety and worry try to pull you into an imaginary horrible future and ruin the present moment. During a crisis, it is important to be able to get outside, play, laugh, cry, and help make an abnormal situation as normal as possible. This is where consistency and routine can help you add a little predictability to your day.

What is in Your Toolbox?

As a therapist, I frequently talk with clients about the coping skills that do and do not work for them. An important thing to remember with choosing a "tool" from your "toolbox" is making sure that it matches the problem. For example, if I have a major loss in my family, deep breathing is not going to be effective for that situation. I may need to cry, talk with someone, or go for a walk. While deep breathing and listening to music are very effective tools for me when I am stuck in Northern Virginia traffic. You can't use a screwdriver to pound a nail. Obtaining and selecting the appropriate coping skills is critical. Coping skills are the things we do to manage the stuff that's going on in our life. Sometimes counselors will talk about it being our toolbox. There are lots of different types of coping skills including self-soothing, distraction, mindfulness, and having a crisis plan. If affirmations do not work for you, try adding, "What if" in front of the statement. I first heard about this from @TikToktraumadoc on Tik Tok, calling them "if-firmations". Affirmations can sometimes feel as though you are trying to believe a lie and they do work for some people. "If-firmations" can sometimes be accepted easier by your conscious and subconscious mind. There are some people that cannot believe or say, "I am beautiful"; however, they can tolerate saying, "What if I am beautiful". It opens the door to curiosity and searching for any evidence that matches that thought. It also helps combat all-or-nothing thinking. "I am" statements are in the affirmative while "what if" statements open the possibility that a piece of the statement may be true. Here is a chart with examples of converting affirmations to iffermations.

AFFIRMATION	"If-fermation"
I am safe.	What if I am safe?
I am worthy.	What if I am worthy?
Everything is going to be ok.	What if everything is going to be ok?
I am loved.	What if I am loved?

Let's Just Cancel Emotions

Often on social media people want to cancel emotions to escape emotional pain. Putting an emotion on hold for a brief period of time is different from canceling the ability to feel. Feelings help us connect with ourselves and others. Emotions can be very uncomfortable, distressing, overwhelming, and even painful at times. Avoiding emotions, pushing them down, and suppressing them is like playing a game of Jack in the Box. The emotions may stay down but they will 'pop-up' unexpectedly. In my experience, the emotions end up exploding in situations that do not warrant that intensity of those emotions. This often leaves the individual and the people around them confused and they may distance themselves from emotions even more. Distancing yourself from emotions and suppressing can show up as the following:

- Distressing dreams
- Agitation
- Misdirected anger
- Physical symptoms (headache, stomachache, chest pain,…)

- Physical illness

This is where I really lean on Dialectical Behavior Therapy (DBT) skills, developed by Dr. Marsha Linehan, to help clients learn how to practice mindfulness, increase frustration tolerance, and learn how to manage their emotions. My favorite part about this approach is the lack of judgment. Many people that struggle with emotion regulation feel that they are 'crazy' and have little hope that they will ever be able to manage their emotions. Instead of telling them to just change their thoughts (which is common in cognitive approaches like Cognitive Behavior Therapy), DBT skills view them as having a skills deficit. Often people that have the most difficulty managing their emotions, have very complicated pasts. When you are surviving, your learning brain shuts down and you just get through it the best you can. Often my clients feel validated when we talk about the fact that they are doing the best they can. Then we can explain how the problem is that their current best is still harming their relationships, themselves, and/or their desired future.

Parenting in a Pandemic

Parenting is actually one of the greatest responsibilities we have, and a crisis can stretch families to their limit. In 2020, many families did not have a buffer between work, school, and home. Everything was happening at the same time and families had to adjust. One of the things I encouraged the parents and families I worked with was to give one another grace and be flexible. Each family has had to do what was best for them. One of the hardest decisions we made was to keep our child in daycare throughout the pandemic. There were two times when we kept him home due to someone testing positive at the daycare, but overall, we were able to keep to our normal routine. My husband worked from home and was able to help out more with parenting tasks and we balanced responsibilities when our son did have to stay home. This meant picking up some hours on Saturday, working later, and making last-minute adjustments.

During the pandemic, I started doing therapy with more adults than children. I understood that if the parents are ok, the majority of the children will be ok. Parents help to ground emotions and give children a safe and secure base. You will also hear this discussed as co-regulation where the parent models regulation and helps their child by first regulating their own emotions. The emotions of our children have an impact on us as parents and that is ok. The key is to not let that trigger a reaction, and instead to respond to their behavior. It is also important to create felt safety and I echoed the advice to tell children that we are not 'stuck' at home, we are 'safe' at home.

Here are some additional tips for parents:

1. Have a plan for when, not if, a crisis happens. Know who you would call and what you would do if there was a shortage of food, housing, gas, etc. Try to save if you can, to prepare for the unexpected.
2. Have a plan for school/daycare closures.
3. Manage your emotions on your own. If you have a partner or consistent help with caregiving, tag them in if you need to take a break to calm/manage an emotion.
4. Model growth mindset and positive thinking, while also validating that the situation is frustrating and disappointing (or any other emotions your children are experiencing).
5. Monitor your children for significant emotional distress. Often children and teens will show this through their behavior. Seek support from the school, medical doctor, or a therapist if you have concerns.

6. Empathize with your children from their perspective. Try not to say, "Well at least you… situation X…" That is invalidating and often tells the other person that their feelings are not valid. Another way to encourage positive thinking would be to say, "I know this year has been rough, what has the hardest part been? What has the best part been?" Many parents implement this on a daily basis by asking their children what was the best and worst part of their day. A friend of mine asks her kids about their 'glows' and 'grows'.

7. Create as much safety, stability, and consistency within the home as you can. For some people, that means developing a flexible routine. A routine can help your child have some predictability in their day.

8. Give your child age/developmentally appropriate information, choices, and some control. There will be a lot that they do not have control over during a pandemic which will make them long for control in their day. For example, they can help plan for the week, choose their clothes (out of appropriate options), decide if they take their bath/shower before or after dinner, etc. Also, have natural consequences when issues arise with your children.

9. Do what works best for your family and do not compare yourself to others. Spend quality time together and also set aside places and times to get breaks as well.

10. Ask for help and support if you need it! There is nothing wrong with needing help, we can all use a little support sometimes.

11. Make sure that you pour into yourself so that you can pour into your children. Engaging in your own self-care is important so that you can be a support for your family.

12. Remember that you are not "just a parent" and try to engage in some hobbies and things you enjoy too.

Can I tell you a little secret that most people do not want you to know? There is always going to be a crisis, there is always going to be something that happens that you do not want or plan for. These recommendations can help you pull through your situation and support your family's needs.

The transition back to the 2021-2022 school year may be difficult for some children, so many of the recommendations listed above may aid in the transition. I am recommending that my families start transitioning their children back to a school year schedule at least two weeks before the school year due to many of our local schools having later start times for the 2020-2021 school year. There will be some uncertainty with the new school year and preparing our children for that can be important. Especially for children that are neurodivergent. I often recommend that parents ask their children to show them their homework instead of asking if they completed it. This attempts to help reduce the opportunity to lie. Also, parents should ensure solid communication with the teacher and school about any concerns or issues. Remember that you all are getting through the crisis together and everyone responds to stress in different ways.

Let's Talk Expectations

Going back to the analogy of driving in a storm from Chapter 1, you may have to adjust your speed during the storm. During 2020, a lot of people were forced to rest due to not being able to go on vacation, to the movies, or participate in extracurricular activities. During an active storm, the goal is to get through as best you can. During 2020, people were worried about children's grades and if they were learning. As a psychologist, I knew that many students would struggle to learn due to the changes, and others would excel. Try to not compare and give yourself permission to make mistakes. With parenting, if you realize that your child is falling short of expectations—calmly have a talk with them, ask them for their input to solve the problem, and give natural consequences if needed. Also, remember to be flexible, what worked in April 2020, may not work in August 2021.

RESOURCES

- *Anxious Kids, Anxious Parents: 7 Ways to Stop the Worry Cycle and Raise Courageous and Independent Children* by Reid Wilson, Lynn Lyons LICSW
- Free E-Book *Playing With Anxiety (*companion book for kids and parents for *Anxious Kids, Anxious Parents)* www.playingwithanxiety.com

REFERENCES

Anxious Kids, Anxious Parents: 7 Ways to Stop the Worry Cycle and Raise Courageous and Independent Children: Wilson, Reid, Lyons LICSW, Lynn. (2013).

Linehan MM, Schmidt HI, Dimeff LA, et al. *Dialectical behavior therapy for patients with borderline personality disorder and drug-dependence. Am J Addict.* 1999; 8: 279–92.

CHAPTER 4

TURNING PAIN INTO PURPOSE

"Purpose is not a destination; it is an ever-evolving journey."

—Dr. Patrice Berry

The year 2020 was one of the greatest and most difficult years of my life. It was the year that I walked away from an agency that I had worked with for over 15 years. I left the certainty of a salaried position and dove into the uncertainty of opening my own private practice. There were many times that I cried and I'm even getting teary-eyed just thinking back to that time. Walking away from my team after schools closed and my position ended was one of the hardest things I have ever done in my career. And at the same time, walking into my own practice was one of the highlights of my career. Selecting an office space, picking out my new furniture, choosing a name and designing the website, and even opening my own bank account. To this day, I do not think I would have left my former position without it ending the way it did (schools closing due to COVID-19 in March 2020). I also did not know the freedom I would feel to fully walk in my purpose within my business and on social media. Once I left, I realized that I had been holding parts of myself back in an attempt to not offend and negatively impact our yearly contract with the school system.

A crisis has the potential to leave you confused and questioning your purpose and goals. However, a crisis can also bring clarity to your priorities and goals for yourself, your family, and your community. The path you choose depends on your perception of the events, flexibility, available resources, and ability to problem-solve. Access to available resources was listed because my decision to leave my job is very different from a single parent needing to maintain full-time employment with benefits to provide for their family. I am married, our insurance is through my husband, and my student loans being on hold gave us the financial cushion we needed to launch the business.

Through my work with survivors and reading the work of Viktor Frankl, a Holocaust survivor, I learned the importance of helping my clients find purpose. Frankl developed logotherapy, an existential analysis to help people find meaning after a tragedy. He says, "Those who have a 'why' to live, can bear with almost any 'how'" (Frankl, 1984). In chapter 1 we discussed learned helplessness, an attitude and mentality that often comes out of extreme pain and struggle. It tells you that nothing you do matters, so why even try. Too much pain (emotional or physical) can give people a shortened sense of the future. With my trauma survivors, I often describe it as an inability to see beyond your nose. While mindfulness grounds you in the present moment, learned helplessness says, "this is all there is so why try or be concerned about more".

Where is Your Control?

Following a crisis, people can either develop a survivor or a victim identity. This is similar to the growth or fixed mindset discussed in an earlier chapter. Someone with a victim identity struggles to accept responsibility for their behavior and blames things on other people. They are typically described as having an external locus of control, where they feel that nothing they do matters and that they have no control over their life. Someone with a survivor identity believes that their life is determined by their choices and accepts responsibility for their actions. Someone with a survivor identity learns to turn their pain into purpose in spite of, and often because of, what has happened in the past. There are children growing up now that are interested in becoming doctors, nurses, teachers, lawyers, firefighters, policemen, or counselors because of what they experienced in 2020. Survivors find ways to look through the pain and discover their purpose.

Discovering your purpose is a journey, not a destination. So, a child who thinks they want to become a doctor in 2021, may discover their true passion for mechanics in five years. Thinking about your purpose and thinking about the future helps us get out of our survival brain and intentionally think three months, six months, one year, or five years down the road. For some survivors, we start with thinking one or two days down the road if they are struggling to think beyond the present moment. There are also times that a person is emotionally very depressed or very anxious and supporting them in their current state is what is best. Thinking about the future can be frustrating and overwhelming, likely because of uncertainty and unanswered questions. It is important to not include issues related to equity in this discussion of internal versus external locus of control. Systemic issues related to race, ethnicity, sex, gender, sexual orientation, and socioeconomic status continue to impact people on a daily basis. In those situations, I still encourage people to advocate for change, focus on what they can control, and receive support for any past wounds.

Where Do I Start?

1. **Stop Avoiding**: Avoidance is an effective short-term strategy to escape feeling emotion for a brief period of time. Problems can arise when we are always running from and avoiding thinking about the future. Thinking about the future can be very scary and often people worry about making the wrong choice, not being good enough, not being successful, or failing to reach their desired goal. This is why we discussed vulnerability earlier. It is going to take vulnerability and courage. I will also be honest and say, you may not reach your desired destination, but what if you do? You will never know if you do not try. It is so easy to not do things, so we will discuss strategies to overcome self-sabotage in the next chapter.

2. **Self-Discovery:** Discover your strengths and your areas for needed growth. If you have difficulty identifying your strengths, ask trusted friends and family to pick two positive words that best describe you. You can also look at a character traits list online and circle the words that describe you now in the present and the words that you want to describe you in the future. In therapy, I sometimes have clients identify words that described them in the past to evaluate how they have grown and changed over time or in treatment. Identify who you are and what you stand for/your values.

3. **Find Your WHY:** Your purpose is often connected to your 'why'. There are lots of different ways to explore this, find the one that works best for you. Some people journal and are able to explore their 'why' through free writing. Some people ask themselves a series of questions like, what do I enjoy doing, what am I great at, what am I passionate about, and what value do I add.

4. **Stay Focused:** If you are really good at a lot of things, it can be easy to get distracted by other tasks. I enjoy dancing and could teach dance lessons; however, that does not connect to my purpose. I was excited to create content on Tik Tok because it gave me a creative outlet for my dancing. Do not compare your journey to other people. That is extremely difficult, and the thoughts of comparison will run rampant in your mind. When that happens, remind yourself of how far you have come. Also, remember that you are only seeing a snapshot of someone else's business or life and do not know what it cost them.

5. **Connect with Like-Minded People/Find a Mentor:** You do not want to be the smartest and most successful

person in your social circle. When that happens, the people around you typically do not understand the choices that you make and may encourage you to go against your stated purpose for short-term benefit. Connect with people who are more successful than you and help support others who are trying to get to where you are. I provide free mentoring through my public social media and then also provide individualized coaching for therapists looking to grow professionally and personally. I have enjoyed connecting with other professionals on Tik Tok and Clubhouse (audio-only live social media app) and have learned so much from others.

6. **Make Decisions and Lead From the Scar and Not the Wound:** Clubhouse was the first place I heard people talking about speaking from the scar and not the wound. When we lead from the wound, we make decisions out of survival brain. When we lead from the scar, we leverage the lessons learned and turn the pain into purpose. After a major loss in my family, I began making tutus for little girls. It was something I did for free for friends and was a healthy outlet for my grief.

7. **Move with the Storm Instead of Against It:** This is where the Dialectical Behavior Therapy (DBT) skill Radical Acceptance really helped me. The saying, "it is, what it is" was my mantra for 2020. Please remember that acceptance is not approval. I can accept the present and actively work to change it. Often we try to fight reality and acceptance is one of the first steps to work towards your desired future. It was heart-crushing to finally hear that schools were closing in March 2020. There was a part of me that knew the decision was coming and actively planned for it. That preparation did not make it hurt any less. "At the same time"

is another phrase from DBT because it helps us hold two contrary emotions simultaneously. I experienced some of the best and at the same time some of the worst months of my life in 2020. Accepting reality helped me to grieve what was lost and work towards my future.

8. **Be Thankful for the Closed Door:** Sometimes a door/opportunity closes that we would have never shut ourselves. It is ok to feel and express your disappointment, just try not to stay there for too long. I like the saying, "When one door closes another one opens." For some people, their life has seen door after door closing, which can make it difficult to have hope that there will be something good that happens. This is where practicing gratitude, focusing on what you can control, and letting go of what you cannot control, can help you problem-solve your way into a better future. There have been many times in therapy where clients were experiencing burnout or joblessness and we used a portion of the time to search for jobs. People with significant depression often struggle to complete tasks, so using a portion of therapy to talk about and search for jobs can be helpful.

9. **Focus on Something Bigger than You:** It is easy to get caught up in what is going on in our lives. Donating your time or resources to local, national, or global organizations can help you develop a greater sense of purpose. This may also help you discover what area/issue you would like to impact. If you are a spiritual or religious person, using prayer, meditation, and seeking spiritual guidance can be helpful to plan your next move. When I was younger I thought that people had one calling and now I realize that we each have a growing, changing, and evolving 'calling'. I never thought that I would have almost 25,000 followers on

a social media app and yet I have an amazing community on Tik Tok. I did not join Tik Tok to be an influencer, I joined to provide mental health information and break the stigma related to seeking help and support. It brightens my day when someone comes back to my page and lets me know that they were able to find a therapist. This positive feedback helps when I receive comments from people attempting to troll my page. They obviously missed my video on 'my page, my content… delete comment'.

Be careful with who you share your purpose and goals. Not everyone will be supportive of your plans and what you hope to accomplish. Learn to trust yourself and value your ideas. External validation and approval from others can feel amazing and I hope that you can find a supportive group of people to help you along your journey. At the same time, everyone may not be supportive of your dream. Continue to press forward and pursue your goals. Internal validation and approval are an amazing gift that you give yourself.

Purpose as a Parent

As a parent, one of the best things you can do is heal your wounds, so they are not passed on to your children. Having a child will show you the areas that you can grow. I thought I was becoming more patient until my child turned three years old. No one warns you about three (mostly joking, but not really). At three years old, children have language and new feelings that they do not know how to express appropriately. From approximately two to six years old, children are known to have irrational moments. For example, your child may have a tantrum about being given the banana that they asked for. In those moments, parents have to take a breath and avoid yelling or shaming statements. All children will make mistakes.

It is a parent's role to provide appropriate boundaries, love, and consequences when your child makes a mistake. I will never forget when our son was two years old, I was cooking, and he was playing quietly. I looked over and he had used a whiteboard marker to draw all over the wall. I knew he had the marker and was drawing on the whiteboard on the refrigerator. Did I yell at him? No, I took a deep breath and remembered that it is my job to watch and teach him. He did a normal thing that kids do, he tested a boundary. Once I was calm (was thinking about painting that wall a different color anyway), I came down to his level and said, "we only draw on the board, we do not draw on the wall". Did he draw on a wall again? Yes, about six months or a year later. This time, a Sharpie fell out of my pocket during bedtime routine and our son drew on the window and windowsill. In case you needed to know, rubbing alcohol will remove Sharpie from a window… and I hope you never need that piece of information. Our son left the Sharpie in the hallway, so when I came upstairs to go to bed, I knew there was a problem. I went into his room and could not see any major marks, so I kissed him on the forehead and went to bed. The very next morning I calmly asked him, show me where you drew last night. He happily took me to both windows. Once again, I had to take a really deep breath, at this point I did not know how to get Sharpie off a window. The most important thing was not the window, it was teaching our son a lesson about our house rules. I came down to his level and calmly let him know that we did not draw on windows or walls. He helped me clean up what he could (just with water and a paper towel). As a parent, I want our son to learn how to problem-solve, manage his emotions and behavior, and always know that he can come to us when he makes a mistake.

    Families can grow closer or further apart during a crisis. A lot of people filed for divorce and a lot of people got married in 2020. Developing a shared purpose as a family can be helpful. As parents (if you are co-parenting), you can determine what you want to be intentional about instilling in your children. Here are some example questions that you may decide to cover in a family meeting:

1. What is my favorite thing about my family?

2. What is one thing that I would change about my family?

3. What is one thing I can do to improve my family? (focus on self and not what other people can do)

4. What goal would I like to accomplish as a family in the next year?

5. What is respect and how can we show respect to one another? (e.g., no yelling, no cursing, no shaming, no tattling on someone to get them in trouble, ask for help) Other examples can be found online by searching "family rules". It is important that everyone including the parents follow these rules.

During crises, families can see an increase in conflict. As parents or caregivers, it is important to present a united front to your children. People often get mad at the children for asking mom and not getting the answer they wanted and going to ask dad. If you know your children do this, send a quick message to mom before you answer. Communication helps to squash manipulation (attempts to get needs met in inappropriate ways). If you have a complicated relationship with your child's other parent, then consider looking into parallel parenting. Co-parenting is where we agree to have similar rules in both houses, and we can communicate on important issues when needed. Parallel parenting is letting go of trying to control what happens in the other person's house as long as the children are safe. With sibling conflict, it can be important to distinguish between tattling and reporting (there are some great images online if you want a visual reminder). Tattling is providing information to get someone else in trouble while reporting is providing necessary information that could impact someone's safety.

Conclusion

Sometimes our purpose comes out of the pain. This does not take away all the pain and most would prefer to just not feel pain at all. Giving pain a purpose can help you survive and thrive during and after the storm. Pain with no purpose can often feel like torture. Sometimes to survive the pain we pick up habits that end up getting in the way of our goals. The next chapter will explore how to overcome self-sabotage and imposter syndrome.

RESOURCES

- *Man's Search for Meaning* by Viktor E. Frankl
- *The Post-Traumatic Growth Guidebook: Practical Mind-Body Tools to Heal Trauma, Foster Resilience and Awaken Your Potential* by Arielle Schwartz
- *Safe People: How to Find Relationships that are Good for You and Avoid Those That Aren't* by Henry Cloud and John Townsend
- *Struggle Well: Thriving in the Aftermath of Trauma* by Ken Falke, Josh Goldberg
- *The Will to Meaning: Foundations and Applications of Logotherapy* by Viktor E. Frankl
- *The Road Back to You: An Enneagram Journey to Self-Discovery* by Ian Morgan Cron, Suzanne Stabile
- *Find Your Why: A Practical Guide for Discovering Purpose for You and Your Team* by Simon Sinek, David Mead, Peter Docker

REFERENCES

Frankl, V. E. (1984). *Man's search for meaning: An introduction to logotherapy*. New York: Simon & Schuster.

Rotter, J. B. Generalized expectancies for internal versus external control of reinforcement. Psychological Monographs, 1966, 80, No. 1

CHAPTER 5

AVOIDING SELF-SABOTAGE & IMPOSTOR SYNDROME

Sometimes the biggest obstacle to achieving our goals is our own thoughts and behaviors. Being aware and understanding the role that self-sabotaging behaviors play in our lives can help us break this cycle. In the midst of a crisis, we often revert to old habits and old ways that meet our needs in the short term at the peril of our future goals. For example, in the midst of the pandemic substance use, emotional eating, and other problematic coping strategies increased. Survival brain can kick in and we go into autopilot. Sometimes we develop behaviors and traits that helped us survive negative events in the past and they no longer serve our current situation. For example, a child growing up in a chaotic environment needs to stay hyper-vigilant, always looking for the bad. However, as an adult in a safe and loving relationship, some people continue to seek out the bad and struggle with accepting peace.

Story Time

This writing process seems to work best when I am totally honest. The person who has been the biggest obstacle to my success is me. I get in my own way all the time and set limits on my success, typically out of fear. I thought it would be helpful to say this because many would not believe this if they met me. My family and friends know the real me! Please know that this chapter comes from real lessons that I have learned and continue to learn along the way. This seems like a good time to talk about the journey to this completed book.

The idea for this book came almost a year ago and I had planned to release it in December 2020. Then our son's daycare shut down, so I planned to release it in March. Then life continued to happen, and I planned to maybe release it in May or June. Oh my, this book has to be done by a speaking engagement where the book will be featured on July 17th! It is currently July 4th and I have 7 of the 12 chapters complete with a deadline to have the book to my editor by tomorrow night. The book has been about 70- 80 percent done for weeks and I am finally setting aside time to get it done! I've always been one to procrastinate and wait until the last minute. Honestly, some of my best work has been in the last hour. I can admit that this time it did not stress me. I planned ahead knowing that I would likely have a big chunk to complete at the end and developed a few shortcuts to work smarter and not harder (one of my favorite sayings).

Procrastination or Self-Care

This is the story of my life because, please believe, I enjoyed every moment that I was not writing this book. I am not sure I can count everything I did as self-care. There was a lot of procrastination. I try to practice what I preach and let go of "should". There are lots of videos and blogs about turning your "should" into "I want to" and your "sorry" into "thank you". For example, instead of saying "I should have started this book weeks ago", saying "I want to start the book". I am not able to change the past and wallowing in what I did not do will not help and often increases negative feelings about the task that needs to be completed. As I typed my "should" statement I even shook my head thinking "I know, I know". I used a sound on Tik Tok that talked about there being a thin line between procrastination and self-care. Here are some tips to manage procrastination:

1. Do NOT wait until you feel like doing it! Just get it done! With my clients that have fitness goals, we talk about not waiting until they feel like going to the gym or until they feel like eating more vegetables and drinking more water, to just complete the task they want.

2. Limit distractions. There were times that I felt like writing, and I did and there were lots of times that I did not feel like it and I distracted myself with Tik Tok, Netflix, Hulu, or various games on my phone. In order to get some chapters completed yesterday, I had to turn off my phone. The temptation to check to see if there were any comments online or just browse is very strong.

3. Remove barriers to completing tasks. Something that really helped me with the writing process was to go back through some old content and pick out quotes and ideas to spark more writing on certain topics. With clients, we talk about setting out their workout clothes and getting everything ready so that when they wake up in the morning all they have to do is put on the clothes and they can complete their desired task.

4. Find ways to make tasks fun. Listening to music or giving myself a little reward can be helpful for completing tasks. I like to admit that the intrinsic feeling of completing the task is not always enough to overcome my desire to NOT do it. It is so hard to do things sometimes. So sometimes saying that I get to do ___ when I complete ___ can be really helpful.

5. Get someone, or a few people, to act as accountable partners and check in with them regularly. I could have hired a relative to edit my book, but I intentionally hired someone outside of my family. I really love the saying that 'lack of preparation on your part does not constitute an emergency on my part'. With a relative, I would have tried to push the deadline and shortened the amount of time they had to review the book prior to publishing. Being accountable to someone who will support, encourage, and challenge you can be key.

Opinions of Others

Sometimes we value the opinion and applause of others more than our own opinion. It is great to receive positive feedback and it feels good. There will also be times when you do not get the feedback that you crave, and you will need to self-validate. You will need to be able to say, I know I did a good job, or I know I did my best. It can also be important to evaluate if the people closest to you and your dream are supportive. There is a big difference between feedback and criticism. Feedback is "maybe you should take a look at your logo, I think you may have made a spelling error. Criticism is "how can any business owner get a logo and not check the spelling. You have an error in your logo, what is wrong with you?". Critical people often have their own issues in their own lives, and they will project that onto you. You will want to limit your time around these types of critical voices if you can. There are times when feedback can feel like criticism when you are in a sensitive or emotional space. If you start to feel negative emotions about the feedback, take a breath, step back, see if they have a point, and think about how the message was delivered.

Strengths Can Also Be Weaknesses

We all have strengths and weaknesses and there are lots of different ways to assess those traits. A common one that people currently talk about is the enneagram test. There is also the Myers Briggs, Strengthsfinder, and many others that can be found online. Multiple professors from graduate school defined me as conscientious as I read through my internship letters of recommendation. That was not a word that I had ever used to describe myself, but it definitely describes me. I am a person that likes to do things right and complete tasks successfully. I am aware of how others may perceive things and there were times that my conscientiousness almost got in the way of my professional goals. For example, with my Facebook business page, I initially did not send out the invite to all my friends. I do not mind receiving those invites and yet I was not sure how others would perceive it. I made a post instead of encouraging people to follow my page. After a few days and only a few followers, I decided to send out the mass invite to all my friends. I almost went through and unselected people, instead I included them and gave them an opportunity to support me.

Take a look at your strengths and see how they add value to your goals and if there are any downsides that you need to be aware of. For example, someone who is very detail-orientated can be too perfectionistic. Someone who is very laid back may struggle to meet deadlines. Someone who has a very good work ethic may be a workaholic. Awareness of how our strengths can get in the way of our goals helps us be intentional with our thoughts, emotions, and behaviors when obstacles arise.

Boundaries

This may seem like an odd place to put a section on boundaries, yet a lack of boundaries can be a form of self-sabotage. There are many different types including emotional, physical, time, and financial boundaries. Setting healthy boundaries lets us communicate to others what is and is not ok for us. A friend can ask to borrow money, and in a healthy relationship, I should be able to say no. The friend asking did not violate my boundary unless I had previously requested that they not ask to borrow money. Here are some basic examples of the different types of boundaries:

Types of Boundaries	Rigid	Permissive	Healthy
Emotional (knowing where my emotions end, and another person's emotions begin)	Closed to anyone talking about their problems (likely due to an inability to regulate their own emotions)	Allows unlimited emotional dumping	Listens and supports a friend in crisis and does not take on the friend's emotions

Physical (touch, intimacy, property, etc.)	Does not allow anyone to touch them	Allows any touch even if they are not comfortable	Allows appropriate touch from family and friends and sets boundaries with new people
Time (Availability, when it is ok to contact, frequency, duration)	Very rigid schedule that cannot change for anyone	Allows others to rearrange their schedule and their day	Is open to spending time with family and friends and also sets limits around availability and duration
Financial (Borrowing or giving money to others)	Never gives anyone any money for any reason	Gives people money despite broken trust and not being repaid in the past	Is willing to support a friend within a certain limit and is not willing to let people borrow large sums of money

Often after being hurt or experiencing childhood wounds, rigid boundaries can feel very safe. Learning who is safe and who is not safe and the ability to recognize red flags of unhealthy relationships can be very helpful. Frequently, individuals with permissive boundaries were not given the right to say 'no' and that feels unsafe for them. Practicing saying no in minor situations can help you learn to set more healthy boundaries. This is a process and does not happen overnight, so be kind and gentle with yourself along the way. Here are some tips to set boundaries:

1. Communicate them early
2. Communicate them clearly
3. Communicate them regularly
4. Reinforce your boundary by saying 'no', hanging up, or removing yourself from a situation.
5. If someone tries to make you feel back about an appropriate boundary, that is a HUGE red flag! Healthy

relationships are built on trust, safety, and support. If someone does not respect your boundaries, they do not respect you.

Another favorite saying is, "the people that benefited the most from you not having any boundaries will be the most upset by them." Do not allow other people that have not healed to determine your worth or value, or, what you should or should not do.

Perfection Paralysis

What is the one thing that you would do if you were not scared, and I could assure you that you would not fail? Even though I am a very conscientious person, I also can say that a task is "good enough" for my mental health, time, energy, etc. If you wait until it is perfect, someone else may go with your idea first. I am not encouraging you to put out bad content or things that are poorly done. For people that are perfectionists, maybe the lighting is not perfect, but it is good enough. Sometimes perfection paralysis is a fear of failure or even a fear of success. Fear can often get in the way of trying something new, applying for a new job, starting a new business, or completing a difficult task. One of my favorite sayings is to 'do it scared'. Releasing my first book is a very scary task and I am excited to do it anyway!

Impostor Syndrome

Do you ever feel out of place when you are in a group of people? Do you ever feel like everybody else around you is smarter and knows so much more than you? Do you ever feel like a fraud and as though people would not want to be around you if people really knew you? If you answered yes to any of these questions, then you may be dealing with impostor syndrome. To clarify, this is not a clinical diagnosis. There are multiple checklists online that you can take to see if you identify with it. The term "impostor phenomenon" was coined by psychologists Dr. Pauline Clance Dr. Suzanne Imes while studying college students. They found in their work that there are a group of people who are very intelligent and successful, who felt like frauds or fakes. I struggled with impostor syndrome, especially early in my professional career and there are times that thoughts of, "Am I good enough?" pop up to this day. Everyone doubts their competence and abilities at times, the goal is to be able to celebrate your wins and not compare yourself negatively to others. Here are some commons signs of imposter syndrome:

- Difficulty accepting compliments or praise
- Discounting success as luck
- Perfectionist (but never feel good enough)
- Fear of failure
- Lack of confidence
- Dread and/or avoids success
- Constantly comparing self negatively to others
- Avoiding extra responsibilities
- Self-sabotage
- Attribute success to outside/external forces or luck

Five Types of Impostor Syndrome (The 5 Types of Impostors: – Impostor Syndrome, 2011)

1. Perfectionist: This person believes that if they don't do it perfectly, then they feel inept. They do not allow themselves to make mistakes or fall short of their expectations. They may set unrealistic standards for themselves and their team. They struggle to celebrate because anything less than 100% is viewed as not good enough. They often feel as though they are not good enough, despite being very good at what they do. I love Brené Brown's book The Gift of Imperfection for this type.

2. Expert: This person thinks they have to know everything on their own. If they do not know the answer to something, they will feel like a failure. Instead, they can feel proud of what

they do know and become more comfortable saying, "let me check on that" in situations, they do not have the information on hand. On Tik Tok, I sometimes get questions that are outside of my area of expertise. Recently, I was tagged in a video on autism, and someone asked a question. I am not an expert in that area and the person was able to get their answer from another creator. It is good to know your limits and accept that no one knows everything. Some people are experts in their field, and they know a lot, I can guarantee you that they do not know everything.

3. Natural Genius/Soloist: This person thinks they have to do it all by themselves if for any reason they need help or support that they are somehow less capable. It really stinks when you have a boss with this mentality because they're not able to delegate to their team. This is also the person that feels a little insecure in their position and does not want other people to learn what they do. Sometimes they worry about being replaced. So, this is the person that believes that they have to do it all themselves on their own without any assistance. As a supervisor, I have always encouraged a team atmosphere where we work together to accomplish the goal and each person plays their part. It is important to know when to delegate and lean on your team. I love the saying 'collaboration over competition'. You winning does not mean someone else has to miss out or lose.

4. Superwoman/Superman/Superperson: This is the one that I have struggled with in the past. The person that feels that it is their mission to accomplish everything on their list or they are a failure. They want to be able to do it all on their own. They often feel guilt, shame, overwhelmed, and burned out by their responsibilities. Accepting their limits, prioritizing rest and self-care, and being intentional with

their time with friends and family is key. This is why I'm taking a summer break from the podcast. We currently record episodes the day before release and do not have any episodes waiting to be posted. This will give us some time to record episodes to be released later. I also used to spend too much time trying to edit the podcast when "authentic conversation" is right in the intro of every video. Finding ways to embrace your humanity and make sure to meet your basic needs of food, sleep, belonging, health, etc. is key.

5. Great Mind: This is the person who believes that they should be able to do everything quickly, with ease, and with speed. This reminds me of an Aldi store cashier because while they are doing their job quickly, with ease, and speed, I do not like how my items just get thrown into the basket. Often grocery stores time how long it takes cashiers to scan all the items and reward fast times. Some jobs and situations require a lot of effort and often we do not get to see other people struggle. When I post on Tik Tok, my viewers do not know how many times I needed to record the video, how I edited it, and they may not notice if I make a small mistake. As a creator, I know all these things and love talking with other creators about the behind-the-scenes of making content. Especially, people that are honest about how they handle not feeling like creating, running out of ideas, and managing other issues that are out of their control. If I stayed by myself in my bubble, I would assume that everyone else was doing it better and having an easier time than I was and that would not be true.

Here are some things that can cause impostor syndrome:

- Critical parent/teacher/authority figure in childhood
- Negative life events/difficult childhood

- Externalizing "successes" and internalizing "failures"
- Negative comparisons
- Social anxiety
- Problematic thinking patterns

Here are some tips to address Imposter Syndrome:

1. DO NOT compare yourself to others. Or more realistically, when you start comparing yourself negatively to others, think about your positive attributes and the things that you do well.

2. Know yourself. Your strengths and your areas of growth. Self-awareness is key to overcoming impostor syndrome. You can leverage your strengths and get support with/find people that are strong in the areas you are growing.

3. DO NOT try to do it all! Know your limits. Often people burn out when they try to do too much. I will say it here again, Dr. Berry does not do it all. I am glad to have an accountant, a website developer, and to continue to grow my team. I also turn down requests to collaborate that do not fit with my current goals.

4. Celebrate your wins. So often people focus on what they do not have, what they are not, and where they want to go and do not focus on their present. When you have a win, celebrate it. Do not forget to celebrate the wins that feel small. You met a deadline, you received a positive review at work (even if you have a few things to work on), you got a promotion (even if it was not the promotion that you wanted), or you decided to start working on that new business part-time.

5. DO NOT internalize your losses. Accept responsibility for what you can do better and learn from your mistakes. A

minor mistake is not a reason to quit. Some of the best things that have happened to me were the people that did not like me, did not continue services with me, or the jobs I did not get offered. I say, "thank you" for the "no", because I honestly believe that another opportunity will come. I will admit that at times I got a little discouraged for a moment when I saw other creators grow faster than I was growing. At the same time, I am so happy with the content that I put out and the approach I have with my page. I am so thankful for every follower that I do have and look forward to connecting with new followers in the future.

6. DO NOT let someone else's light dim yours. Collaborate, DO NOT compete! It can be intimidating to be around people who have different levels of success. Their success can push you to grow. When I first got on Tik Tok I never thought that I would have people excited when I followed them back. I felt that way when larger creators would check out my content and follow me back. Growth/success always has a downside too, so make sure to be around authentic people who will share the difficult aspects of their journey and not just their Instagram highlights.

7. Surround yourself with people who encourage and support you. Also, with those who encourage you to grow and will give you honest feedback. If you receive feedback, do not get defensive and take it personally. I remember when a larger creator gave me feedback to not duet a video with a black screen. They called it a "lazy duet". I did not get mad about this feedback, I took it and decided to make a change. Before receiving that feedback, a larger creator in my niche told me that my content was a little random. I knew this and I love being random, but that can confuse the algorithm or people may follow you for something that was done on a whim.

Feedback is very different from criticism. Feedback does not mean that you are wrong or that something is wrong with you. There have also been times when I received feedback that did not apply to my life. I will never forget that my college advisor recommended that I become a psychiatrist. Psychiatrists are medical doctors, and I did not want to become a medical doctor. Becoming a psychologist was my path and it was ok to disregard that feedback.

8. Practice self-compassion and positive self-talk. Give yourself a chance to be human, to feel, and to fail. You will not always know the answer and that does not mean that you are dumb. You will not always meet the deadline and that does not mean that you are worthless. You will not always get the job you want and that does not make you less qualified. I recently talked about a job that I was not offered because the interviewer knew that I would not last at the agency. It was a state agency and what I was looking for, they weren't able to offer. I was highly qualified for the position, but I was not the right fit. I would have likely looked for a new job within 1-2 years if I had been offered the job. I believe that the interviewer took into account the cost and time it would've taken to train a new person if/when I would've left, and subsequently decided not to offer me the position.

Building Confidence and Self-Worth

Confidence is how you feel about yourself and is closely tied to your self-talk. People often think very negative things about themselves but think very highly of others. Sometimes people with low confidence put the needs of others in front of their own. If you are a people-pleaser, remember that you are 'people' too. Learn who you are and what you want. It is important to learn how to validate yourself and appreciate your worth and value. As mentioned in a previous chapter, our self-talk is often shaped by our caregivers, family members, and friends. What if they lied? What if you are worthy? What if you deserve to be treated with dignity and respect? What if you have something worthwhile to contribute? Did you see what I did there? Inserted a few of those "if-firmations". I believe that everyone has value and that everyone deserves to be treated with dignity and respect. Even people that have not earned it and people that I strongly disagree with. I also believe that people should be held accountable for their actions if they break the law and/or harm others.

Who or what are you allowing to determine your value? One of my favorite exercises to show someone's value is to take out a $20 bill and show that it still has value even if you fold it, crumple it, stomp on it, or even tear it in half. Despite all that you have been through, you still have value. Your worth and your value did not change just because someone else did not see or recognize it. Sometimes we can question our worth and value when we compare ourselves to others. This is where I would encourage you to run your race and stay in your lane. You do not know what it costs that other person to get to and maintain their station in life. When you find yourself questioning your value, remember that Dr. Berry said that you are worthy, loved, and you get to determine if you will accept your full value. You are not your behavior. You are not what you've been through, there is greater in you.

Success does not make you who you are, it reveals who you are. If you are struggling with confidence as an employee, you would likely struggle with confidence as a boss/manager. Being married, having a child, and/or making your dream salary does not make you happy or successful. Becoming "Dr. Berry" licensed psychologist, did not change who I was, my worth, or my value. It did allow me to operate within my field and I continue to learn and grow. I am just as confident as "Ms. or Mrs. Berry, as I am with Dr. Berry".

As you begin to develop your self-confidence and self-worth, the people around you may try to bring you back down to where you were before. Some people are more comfortable with you having low self-esteem, questioning yourself, and not knowing your true worth. Knowing your worth and value may change your friend group. There are some great quotes about finding out who your true friends are when you fail and when you succeed. I love when my friends win, and I celebrate with them. I also grieve with them when they are down. Sometimes as we are finding ourselves, there is a period of being alone. You can be alone and not be lonely. If you notice that your friend group changes and you do not have as much support, use that time to find yourself and find your voice. I hope that you will eventually find a safe, authentic, and supportive community that you grow in. You are valid, you are worthy, you are more than what you do and who you love. You have value and worth because you are you and there is no one else like you. No one else can do what you are here to do. Stay in your lane and accomplish your goals.

RESOURCES

- www.impostorsyndrome.com
- *Unlocking Your Authentic Self: Overcoming Impostor Syndrome, Enhancing Self-confidence, and Banishing Self-doubt* by Jennifer Hunt
- *Impostor Syndrome Remedy: How to improve your self-worth, feel confident about yourself, and stop feeling like a fraud!* (Psychology in your life Book 2) by Emee Vida Estacio
- *The impostor Cure: Escape the mind-trap of impostor syndrome* by Dr. Jessamy Hibberd
- *The Mindful Self-Compassion Workbook: A Proven Way to Accept Yourself, Build Inner Strength, and Thrive* by Kristin Neff and Christopher Germer

REFERENCES

The 5 Types of Impostors: – Impostor Syndrome. (2011, December 25). Impostorsyndrome.com. https://impostorsyndrome.com/5-types-of-impostors/

CHAPTER 6

HELPERS NEED HELP TOO

"Because true belonging only happens when we present our authentic, imperfect selves to the world, our sense of belonging can never be greater than our level of self-acceptance."
— Brené Brown, **Daring Greatly: How the Courage to Be Vulnerable Transforms the Way We Live, Love, Parent, and Lead**

The people who are the best at giving advice and being there for others are often the worst at asking for and/or receiving help. During all of the events that unfolded in 2020, my thoughts were with the people who were already struggling before the pandemic, the essential workers, parents, teachers, healthcare professionals, and anyone in a helping profession. I appreciate those reminders to check-in on your strong friends because they may need it and not ask for it. In my private practice, I saw an increase in people who were in therapy for the first time. Prior to COVID and all the other events in 2020, they were able to manage their lives with little issue. During my first session with these individuals, I would let them know how happy I was that they were in treatment and that therapy is for the strong. There is so much stigma associated with mental health and accessing help and support, I wanted to normalize and applaud them for seeking therapy.

Vulnerability is NOT Weakness

Brené Brown's work changed my life forever. I had an unhealthy view of vulnerability and being a "strong woman". I was raised by a single mother who seemed to do it all. My mom has been through a lot and never seemed to let any of it phase her. Growing up, I do not remember ever seeing her struggle. Back in the '80s (yes

I know I'm older), Black women were encouraged to not let the world see them struggle. We were encouraged to put on a superwoman cape and conquer all. This is not to throw shade at the people who had to do this to survive their experiences. Vulnerability can definitely feel like a privilege and cannot be used in every situation. For example, if I have a toxic work environment, it would be prudent to be on guard and share very little about my personal life. However, if I am in a supportive work environment and or am struggling, I want to have the ability to ask for help.

My mentality changed to accept that vulnerability is not weakness, it is ok to not be ok, and it is ok to not have all the answers. Often helpers are really good at helping and giving to others but may struggle with receiving help and receiving from others. It takes vulnerability and courage to admit that you are not ok and accept help from others. Vulnerability is the opposite of control because you do not know what the outcome will be. In my experience, helpers like to KNOW and do not like being uncomfortable. Vulnerability is uncomfortable and on the other side of that discomfort is joy, peace, fulfillment, and support. My husband stepped up in big ways for our family over the past 16 months and he did not have to guess what we needed. I asked him to help with dinner and we would set up a schedule that met both of our needs when we had to stay home due to possible COVID exposures at my son's daycare. If you have friends, family, or a partner that will show up for you when you ask, please seek support when you feel like you are drowning. Early in my marriage, I would want my husband to read my mind and see what we needed. It is less stressful to just ask for what I need and not expect him to read my mind.

Oftentimes, one the biggest blockades to people seeking support, is fear. Fear about being rejected, being let down, things not working out the way you want them to or losing a piece of your role within your family/organization. Let's be honest and admit that when you ask for help, you may not receive the exact help you need. At the same time, not asking for help guarantees that you will not receive any. So, let's step beyond fear into courage ,and start with a small request. If it does not go the way you want it to, I would have an honest conversation about what you are needing and see if you can receive any additional help and support. When people are used to you doing it all, they may not jump up at the opportunity to do more. Honestly, the way things currently are works for them, but is leading to burnout for you.

Avoiding Burnout & Compassion Fatigue

Burnout is characterized by exhaustion, cynicism, and detachment due to one or more of the following factors: lack of control over important aspects of your job, being underpaid and overworked, and a toxic work environment including issues with management and/or consumers. (Maslach & Leiter, 2016)

There are physical, mental/cognitive, and emotional signs of burnout including difficulty sleeping, headaches, stomach aches, muscle tension, exhaustion, difficulty completing tasks, difficulty thinking, increasing cynicism, anxiety, and frustration. As a caregiver, you can also become overwhelmed with your responsibilities and role which can trigger feelings of guilt and shame. Acknowledging these feelings is the first step to get help and support. I saw an increase in medical providers and teachers accessing therapy within the past year.

We need to normalize that self-care is NOT selfish. I am convinced that airlines tell passengers to put on their own mask for the overly enthusiastic helpers on the plane who would take care of others before they take care of themselves. The truth is that I am no use to anyone else if I'm passed out. We must always put our mask on first and prioritize self-care and rest. As my friend on Tik Tok @My_Destination says, "rest isn't a reward. It is a prerequisite. Being tired makes you ineffective and if you treat rest as a reward, you may never get rest".

Helpers often get into their work out of their own past pain. Social workers, therapists, police officers, military service members, medical doctors, and nurses often have a painful story that leads them to their profession. For me, it was a bad experience with a middle school guidance counselor. For others, maybe it was growing up with a chronic illness, substance abuse, and/or severe mental illness. It is important to seek support if those old wounds get triggered (as discussed in Chapter 1). There are lots of options with burnout including searching for new employment, finding creative outlets for your emotions (art, crafts, music), exercise, getting more sleep, meditation/spiritual practice, and practicing gratitude. While you are in your current position that you may hate, trying to find the good in your current circumstance.

Compassion fatigue can often be resolved quicker than burnout. Compassion fatigue is where you enjoy your work; however, it is beginning to take a toll. I have heard some people describe it as caring too much. As a beginning therapist, I took responsibility for my client's progress and felt like a bad clinician if someone did not get better. During training and supervision, I realized that the client's progress was their own and I needed to meet them where they were. For some individuals, progress may be them developing a trusting relationship with a therapist and nothing else may change in a significant way. I realized that I cannot change them, it was my job to provide resources and tools and it was on my client to use them. I love giving this message to parents as well. Often parenting is filled with attempts at control instead of teaching and guidance. For some of my clients, they would need a higher level of care (short-term or long-term out of home placement, intensive home-based therapy) or they may need a different type of treatment. Focusing on my strengths and allowing my clients to own their progress helped relieve a lot of the stress I felt. If the day comes when someone shares something painful with me and I feel nothing, I will quit psychology. I must empathize with my clients, but I have tools and resources I use to maintain healthy boundaries and not take their problems home with me. One of my friends, Rosa Jones (@rosajoneslpc) describes codependence as "over-functioning in their life and under-functioning in my own". This is why it is important that helpers do their own work and heal/receive healing for their own wounds.

Set Boundaries

As discussed in Chapter 5, boundaries are an important part of self-care. Emotional boundaries in particular are key in avoiding compassion fatigue and burnout because they separate my emotions from the emotions of others. People who describe themselves as empaths often take on the emotions of others and it is important for empathic people to learn how to disconnect from the energy of others. Techniques that work for me include monitoring the tension in my body and my breath. I will often take a breath with a client as they share something really difficult. Emotional boundaries are knowing where my emotions end, and someone else's emotions begin. Carrying the emotions of others is not effective. Teaching someone how to carry their own emotions is much more helpful. In my experience, people are not equipped to carry the emotions of others for extended periods of time. I can support without taking on all of the emotion. For spiritual people, the only person that can carry the weights and burdens of others is God. When we try to do that for people, we end up becoming their 'god' and it typically ends up hurting both people.

One of my favorite boundaries to use is the word 'no', remembering that no is a complete sentence. It does not require an explanation and yet when you start setting boundaries in your life some people will misinterpret the mere existence of boundaries for you being mean. These are the individuals that need your new boundaries the most. People will attempt to cross your boundary and it is your job to reinforce it. When I used to work for a larger agency, if my boss would come to me and say that she needed something by a certain date, I would ask for assistance with something that was already on my plate or make a recommendation to reprioritize what was currently on my plate.

Self-Care

As a therapist, I listen to the darkest and most painful parts of people's lives, and managing my own emotions is my priority. I have heard horror stories online and in my own office about therapists breaking down when clients share their stories. Now I have shed a tear with a client, for the client amid their pain. However, the client should remain the focus in sessions, and I must remain a source of stability. One of the strategies that I use and teach my clients is to fill their own cup first. Before you can give to others, you must first pour into yourself. Each person does this in their own way. Some people wake up at 5am and exercise, some people meditate first thing in the morning, for me, it is my morning cup of coffee or tea. Then I do little things throughout my day to continue to pour back into myself so I can pour into others. There is also a phenomenon that I have seen with children, teens, and adults where no matter how much is poured into their cup, they are still empty.

On Tik Tok, @thedorkweb did an amazing video illustrating this with a broken cup. I often explained it this way, 'sometimes it can feel as though someone does not have a bottom on their cup and everything that is poured in falls right out'. In these scenarios, seeking a therapist can be helpful to help repair that cup.

Be sure to take care of your mind, body, and spirit as you pour into and care for others. No one is able to 'do it all' and we all have our limits. It is my recommendation to avoid things like alcohol when you are stressed because it is a depressant and lowers inhibition (thinking before you act). Lastly, remember that you are human and let yourself laugh and cry. Laughter can be one of the best stress relievers and sometimes it can be very helpful to cry when overstressed. For people that have difficulty letting themselves cry, I recommend watching a really sad movie and having a good cry.

Manage Your Expectations and Thoughts

During a workshop that I attended on compassion fatigue facilitated by Dr. Eric Gentry, he talked about the concept of the 'perceived threat'. During the past 16 months, I reminded myself that there is pain and then there is suffering. Pain is inevitable and suffering is impacted by my perception. For example, I am in a lot of Facebook groups and the clinician groups continue to stress out about how long telehealth will be offered. Telehealth (secure video counseling) was offered and paid for by a lot of insurances before the pandemic. In those groups, I would also see therapists complaining about how much they HATED telehealth. I actually enjoy it and was able to launch my business before I secured a physical location due to being able to offer services online. In the midst of caring for others, try to find the things that you enjoy. If you are unable to find anything, you may have 'burnout'. Instead of focusing on everything that was wrong, I looked for opportunities to grow on social media, launched my podcast, and took advantage of opportunities to grow and expand my practice.

Before COVID, I do not think I would have tried telehealth. I preferred in-person therapy until I realized how many people benefit from the option of having services online. I was able to meet with people during their lunch breaks and was able to expand my services across the entire state of Virginia. Telehealth also gives me a glimpse into the real lives of my clients versus how they show up to my office. I will also be honest and admit that my personality is pretty optimistic. Some people are realists or pessimists that may struggle to find the good. This is where practicing gratitude can be really helpful; teaching your brain to look for the good every day, even if it seems very small. It is also important to avoid those 'thought traps' discussed in previous chapters. Catastrophizing and 'all or nothing' thinking are two of the main traps I see during a crisis. Check out Dr. Gentry's YouTube channel for his videos called "Tools for Hope" Part 1 and Part 2, where he discusses his approach.

Part One Conclusion

Congratulations on completing Part 1 of this book, Survival. Now that you have a foundation to survive, we can talk about thriving and building resilience. Even if you feel that you are still in survival mode, there may be tips and tools in the following chapters that can help you along the way. Resilience is something that can be developed within all of us, it is not a trait that certain people possess. Let's continue along this journey together and learn how to shift out of survival mode and into thrive mode, getting better and stronger each day.

RESOURCES:

- *Forward-Facing(R) Professional Resilience: Prevention and Resolution of Burnout, Toxic Stress and Compassion Fatigue* by J Eric Gentry PH D and Jeffrey Jim Dietz M D

REFERENCES

Maslach, C., & Leiter, M. P. (2016). Understanding the burnout experience: recent research and its implications for psychiatry. *World psychiatry : official journal of the World Psychiatric Association (WPA)*, *15*(2), 103–111. https://doi.org/10.1002/wps.20311

PART 2
THRIVE

CHAPTER 7

STRATEGIES TO BUILD RESILIENCE AND THRIVE

In order to learn how to thrive it is imperative that we be clear of immediate danger. Survival comes naturally, even if some of the behaviors are maladaptive at the time. Often, we have to learn new skills, do new things, and possibly surround ourselves with new people to thrive. Whether you are ready to survive or thrive, sharpening your skills can help change how you are currently responding to your storm.

We started the book with more general definitions of survive, "continue to live or exist, especially in spite of danger or hardship" (definition of survive - Google Search, 2011) and thrive, "grow or develop well or vigorously" (definition of thrive - Google Search, 2018). Resilience is defined as, "the process of adapting well in the face of adversity, trauma, tragedy, threats or significant sources of stress" (Building your resilience, 2020).

Post-Traumatic Growth (PTG)

Typically, after a crisis, we hear about post-traumatic stress including the common symptoms that people can experience after a negative life event. Have you heard about post-traumatic growth? This term was first coined in 1996 (Tedeschi & Calhoun, 1996) and the Post-Traumatic Growth Inventory (PTGI) was developed to assess the following areas after a crisis: a newfound appreciation of life, relationship with others, new possibilities in life, personal strength, and spiritual change. After a crisis individuals can be overwhelmed with PTSD symptoms, surviving with some symptoms, show signs of resilience, or showing signs of post-traumatic growth. Wherever an individual is on their healing journey, there is help and support and no judgment. Here is a link to a helpful handout that provides information on support and resources for people after a crisis. https://www.ptsd.va.gov/professional/treat/type/PFA/VA_NCPTSD_All_508.pdf Post-traumatic growth helps survivors see themselves as capable of transformation and change.

Activities that promote PTG in families and young kids:

- Activities that build a sense of security by reassuring children of love and safety
- Consistency/routine
- Parents teaching and modeling coping skills
- Parents managing their reactions
- Providing children with age and developmentally appropriate information
- Parents receiving their own support/therapy when needed/if there is a lack of knowledge about healthy coping

Activities that promote PTG in Teens and Adults:

- Community/social connection-support groups, churches/religious groups, etc.
- Create a safe space for people to safely express and feel their positive and negative emotions
- Poetry
- Music
- Journaling
- Normalize and validate negative emotions and prime them to look for and/or create the positive/meaning-making
- Dialectical Behavior Therapy skills
- Increasing felt safety to reduce hyper-vigilance/threat scanning
- Planning/trying to return to "normal"
- Gratitude
- Internal locus of control

- Replacing unhealthy habits or coping with positive/healthy coping skills
- Practice using coping skills when calm to be able to implement them in crisis. Our brains default to what we are used to practicing and doing in survival mode.
- Breathing and increasing the feeling of control during difficult symptoms

A colleague recommended a great book, *The Obstacle is the Way* by Ryan Holiday as I was launching my private practice in 2020. Oftentimes we get distracted by the obstacles in the road and think we have to go a whole new route. There may be a way through the obstacle or an even better path available because of the obstacle. This is one of the best examples of the growth mindset that we discussed in previous chapters. Seeing the obstacle or the problem and getting clarity on your destiny and purpose. I likely would not have joined Tik Tok if it was not for COVID. I definitely would not be offering telehealth if it was not for 2020. I also saw how conversations about race deepened many relationships and people began to see the inequities in our system for the very first time. I do not think that would have happened if it was not for COVID. There were also a lot of losses and I do not minimize or trivialize that fact. The loss and the pain will be felt for many years and possibly generations to come. It is my hope that we can continue to carry the lessons learned and create a better future for our children and their children.

Emotional Intelligence

Here I will provide a brief overview of emotional intelligence and encourage you to check out the books on this topic if this is an area where you would like to learn additional information. You can also always ask me general questions on YouTube, Tik Tok, and IG in the comments if you have questions on any topics covered in this book. In the '90s Peter Salovey and John Mayer defined emotional intelligence as "the ability to monitor one's own and others' feelings and **emotions**, to discriminate among them and use this information to guide one's thinking and actions" (**Salovey & Mayer**, 1990). Daniel Goleman is the one who most people associate with emotional intelligence due to his book and its application to the workplace. He stressed the importance of having employees who were self-aware, can regulate their emotions, are motivated, have empathy, and have good social skills. His research also found that people with higher levels of emotional intelligence tend to be more successful (Goleman, 1995).

There are a lot of factors that contribute to a person's ability to regulate their emotions and their behavior. If someone is lacking the skills to manage emotions, Dialectical Behavior Therapy (DBT) skills (developed by Dr. Marsha Linehan) can be very helpful. DBT skills are a non-judgmental and validating approach to help people learn to increase their ability to stay in the moment (mindfulness), tolerate difficult events and emotions (distress tolerance), appropriately interact and engage with others (interpersonal effectiveness), and manage their emotions (emotion regulation).

Resilience at Work

Due to unexpected changes within the past year many workplaces are going to attempt to get back to "normal". This may trigger anxiety, worry, and concerns for the employees. Here are some tips to build resilience at work (tips derived from CANVA image):

1. Live authentically: acknowledge your difficulties and your strengths. There will always be aspects of your job that you do not like and things that you do like. Generally, the things that we do not like stand out more than the pleasant parts of our job, especially if we are close to burnout. If you have a supportive work environment, being able to communicate concerns to supervisors/management can be helpful.

2. Build supportive networks: find at least one work associate that you can talk to and get support from if you need to. If you work a mostly solitary job, connecting with family and/or friends can be helpful. Connecting with other people in your field can also help you not feel alone.

3. Manage stress: engage in self-care at home and at work. Set boundaries when needed around work and home. If you are working from home, I recommend setting up a dedicated workspace that is separate from your living space if possible. This helps to give you some separation in your day-to-day life. Even if it is just a desk in your bedroom.

4. Find your purpose/calling: if you are not at your dream job, find an aspect of your job that you enjoy and know that you are making a difference in someone's life. Try not to minimize that impact by saying words like 'I just', 'it is only', or comparing yourself to other people or professions.

5. Maintain perspective: there will be things that you do not like about your work environment. Focus on the things that you do like and practice gratitude. The negative aspects will often stand out and you will have to search for the positive. No matter how small, find the parts of your job that you like. If you are burned out, use that dislike for the job to fuel your search for your next position.

6. Be cooperative with others: have a positive attitude and a collaborative approach with others. Manage your emotions first when coworkers or customers activate your anger, frustration, or anxiety. Focus on what you can control and the things that you are able to do.

RESOURCES

- *DBT Skills Training Handouts and Worksheets, Second Edition* by Marsha M. Linehan
- *Emotional Intelligence: Why It Can Matter More Than IQ* by Daniel Goleman
- *Transformed by Trauma: Stories of Posttraumatic Growth* by Richard G. Tedeschi PhD
- *The Obstacle Is the Way: The Timeless Art of Turning Trials into Triumph* by Ryan Holiday

REFERENCES

Building your resilience. (2020). Building your resilience. Https://www.apa.org. https://www.apa.org/topics/resilience

definition of survive - Google Search. (2011). Google.com.

definition of thrive - Google Search. (2018). Google.com.

Goleman, D. (1995). *Emotional intelligence: Why it can matter more than IQ.* New York: Bantam Books.

Joseph, S., & Butler, L. (2010). Positive changes following adversity. PTSD Research Quarterly, 21 (3), 1–3.

Linehan MM, Schmidt HI, Dimeff LA, et al. Dialectical behavior therapy for patients with borderline personality disorder and drug-dependence. *Am J Addict.* 1999; 8: 279–92.

Salovey, P., & Mayer, J. D. (1990). Emotional Intelligence. Imagination, Cognition and Personality, 9(3), 185–211. https://doi.org/10.2190/DUGG-P24E-52WK-6CDG

Tedeschi, R. G., & Calhoun, L.G. (1996). The Posttraumatic Growth Inventory: Measuring the positive legacy of trauma. Journal of Traumatic Stress, 9, 455-471.

CHAPTER 8

HOLISTIC WELLNESS

Holistic health and wellness have been a passion of mine since I was a teenager. It was my goal, right around the time I realized that I wanted to be a psychologist, to eventually own a holistic health center that housed medical, dental, and counseling professionals in one building so people could get holistic restoration within one location. Those were my childhood dreams before almost $200,000 in student loan debt and a family. Maybe it will still happen in the future, the one thing I do know is that there had to be a section in this book about taking care of your WHOLE self.

Usually someone that takes really good care of their physical health will neglect their mental health and vice versa. In fact, our physical and mental health have a direct impact on each other. Hettler (1976) identified the following six dimensions of wellness: physical, emotional, intellectual, spiritual, occupational, and social wellness. While no one's life will ever be in perfect balance, it can be important to know how you are doing in these areas. I bring this approach to my counseling and if someone is unemployed, part of our session will include discussing any mental health barriers to their job search. If someone has unstable housing, we can use part of our time to research housing options. Clients have canceled sessions due to having job interviews or work schedule changes. Let's take a closer look at those six dimensions of whole-person wellness (Hettler 1976).

Physical wellness includes your physical health and fitness. Exercise can be a great way to manage your physical health and it also benefits your emotional, spiritual, and intellectual wellness too. Find exercise that you enjoy, for example, if you hate running, try doing a more pleasant activity. I enjoy Zumba and any aerobic dance workout. I also know that I do better at the gym or when other people are watching because I will stop working out or not push myself as hard when I am on my own. Physical health also includes nutrition. Feeding your body more of what it needs as opposed to only what it wants.

Emotional wellness includes your mental health and your ability to regulate your emotions. Everyone has to be concerned with mental health/emotional well-being. Emotional wellness focuses on emotional awareness and regulation. Your ability to identify and manage the roots of emotional distress is critical to your emotional wellness. Healthy coping skills and self-care also encourage emotional wellness.

Intellectual wellness includes engaging in tasks that inspire creativity and challenge you mentally. Reading, learning, and doing challenging tasks are examples of ways to build intellectual wellness. When I do not get enough sleep and cannot self-medicate with coffee, my mental wellness is significantly impacted. Intellectual wellness also entails your willingness to be flexible, learn new things, and consider alternate perspectives.

Spiritual wellness includes one's purpose and meaning in life. The individual has a sense of direction in their life and strives to live a life consistent with their beliefs and values. Spiritual wellness can be impacted by all of the other dimensions of wellness. For some people, emotional struggles bring them closer spiritually and for others, it drives them away from spiritual activities.

Occupational/Financial wellness includes an individual's satisfaction with their work and their financial resources. It also includes walking in your purpose and how job dissatisfaction can impact this dimension and other dimensions. I have seen individuals who struggle in this dimension also struggle with spiritual wellness. Especially if they are unclear about their purpose. Once again, purpose is not a destination and constantly evolves and changes.

Social wellness includes connecting and contributing to your community. More specifically, the groups that you are a part of and your ability to connect with other members those groups. It also includes connecting with nature and social activism.

Rate each of these areas of wellness:

Areas of Wellness	1 Very Poor	2 Poor	3 Fair	4 Good	5 Excellent
Physical					
Emotional					
Intellectual					
Spiritual					
Occupation					
Social					

Which area or areas were the highest?
_____

Which area or areas were the lowest?
_____

Which area or areas suffer when stressed?
_____

Think about when you are in a crisis, which area(s) do you seem to thrive in and prioritize, and which area(s) suffer. I know for me; I prioritize my emotional and spiritual wellbeing and can neglect my physical wellness. My body normally tells me when I am starting to feel stressed. I feel the tension building in my neck and lower back, stomach tightness, and rapid heart rate. Identify and practice utilizing the tools that can help you be more intentional in the area(s) that may get ignored or neglected. I also want to note that perfect balance is impossible. There will almost always be an aspect that could use your attention.

Illusion of Work-Life Balance

Many people strive endlessly for work-life balance. Recently, during a conversation with my mom, she discussed how things will never be in perfect balance. There are times that one aspect of your life may need more of your attention, and another may get a little less. The goal is to be intentional with your time and ensure that you are prioritizing things based on urgency and importance. To be honest, during the final push of this book, I was not in perfect balance. I had to step away from going live on Tik Tok, I got a little behind with my billing for my private practice, and my home was a little messier. I knew this was only for a period of time and I have plans to get back on track once this book is complete. And you know what, that's okay!

When I get the question, "Dr. Berry, how do you do it all?" My response is, "I don't". There are things that do not get done. There are times that I have to prioritize sleep, time with my family, or notes and billing. And again, that's okay!

What is on Your Plate?

A common therapeutic intervention is to have a client write down all of their responsibilities on little pieces of paper and place them on a plate. We often discuss how heavy the plate is and there are things that they are carrying that they can take off their plate.

We go through each item and the client decides if it is something that needs to be on their plate. The visual can be very powerful when people look at all the people, responsibilities, worries, concerns, and other emotions that they are carrying. Similar to the forgiveness chapter, there are things that we carry that weigh us down. For example, there are parents that feel responsible for their child's grades. As a parent I am responsible for helping support my child; however, the grades are my child's grades. As a parent, I can take my child's grades off my plate of concerns and place it on their plate. As a parent, I am responsible for teaching my child and yet I am not responsible for my child's behavior. Legally I am responsible, but my child is the one who has to make the choice. Trying to control everything and everyone helps a person reduce their felt-anxiety in the moment, yet it increases their stress and frustration.

Holistic Treatments

There are medical doctors that practice holistic medicine. Locally, there was a practice that would bill insurance for a portion of services (general physical and certain laboratory results) and then we would pay out of pocket for the tests that were not covered. In my own life, a holistic doctor was able to diagnose and treat an issue that I had for years in a matter of months. Here are some examples of holistic treatments (many are not covered by insurance):

- Acupuncture
- Chiropractor
- Naturopathy
- Reflexology
- Herbal medicine
- Aromatherapy
- Massage
- Meditation

*This is for information only and not a recommendation. Be sure to check the licensure and validity of treatment providers before requesting services. Discuss concerns with a medical doctor.

Why the WHOLE Person?

I have always been concerned about treating the whole person because when a client comes in, they do not just come in with their mental and social wellness. The entire person enters my office, and it is my goal to connect them with resources to address their concerns. Taking a whole person approach often helps clients feel validated and see the value of the overall wellness during their mental health treatment. They are able to bring their whole selves into treatment to receive support. As a psychologist, I cannot advise them in every area, but I can point them to helpful and valuable resources.

RESOURCES:

- *Think and Grow Rich: The Original, an Official Publication of The Napoleon Hill Foundation* by Napoleon Hill
- *The Sleep Revolution: Transforming Your Life, One Night at a Time* by Arianna Huffington
- *Thriving with Adult ADHD: Skills to Strengthen Executive Functioning* by Phil Boissiere MFT
- *Faith That Hurts, Faith That Heals/Understanding the Fine Line Between Healthy Faith and Spiritual Abuse* by Jack Arterburn, Stephen; Felton
- *The Subtle Power of Spiritual Abuse: Recognizing and Escaping Spiritual Manipulation and False Spiritual Authority Within the Church* by David Johnson and Jeff VanVonderen
- *When Narcissism Comes to Church: Healing Your Community From Emotional and Spiritual Abuse* by Chuck DeGroat and Richard J. Mouw
- *God Can't: How to Believe in God and Love after Tragedy, Abuse, and Other Evils* by Thomas Jay Oord
- *Escaping the Maze of Spiritual Abuse: Creating Healthy Christian Cultures* by Lisa Oakley and Justin Humphreys
- *Healing Spiritual Abuse: How to Break Free from Bad Church Experience* by Ken Blue

- *Broken Trust: …a practical guide to identify and recover from toxic faith, toxic church, and spiritual abuse (The Overcoming Series: Spiritual Abuse, Book 4)* by F. Remy Diederich
- *A Year of Self-Care: Daily Practices and Inspiration for Caring for Yourself* by Dr. Zoe Shaw

REFERENCES

Hettler, B. (1976). Six dimensions of wellness model.

CHAPTER 9

COPING WITH GRIEF & LOSS

Coping with grief and loss is something rarely discussed in mainstream society, specifically in America. There are cultures that have specific rituals following a loss. My approach to grief changed after experiencing a significant loss because I understood it in a whole new way. It had been a while since I had dealt with a significant personal loss. My grief was very overwhelming at first and I stopped working with people who were currently experiencing grief or sought supervision for cases that I was currently working on to make sure I was able to fully support my clients. The feeling of knowing that there is nothing you can do to take someone else's pain as you experience your own grief is extremely weighty. I found peace and support in my faith and in my family. There are people that draw away from their faith in times of grief and this is completely understandable. I hope the section on toxic faith helps to support why this can happen at times. I was grateful to be a part of a church that allowed space for grief and anger at God.

There are a lot of different types of grief and loss including pet loss, child loss, unexpected, and expected losses. One of my favorite quotes to share with individuals grieving is "Grief is just love with no place to go" by Jamie Anderson. When working with individuals who are grieving I encourage them to express their hurt and also process the love. It can be difficult for the griever to 'move forward', as it can carry a connotation of leaving something or someone behind. So, we often talk about 'moving through" the grief instead.

Tips for People Who Are Grieving

1. Let yourself feel when it is safe. You will likely feel a range of complicated emotions. There is no right or wrong way to feel. There may be times that you feel like crying, times you want to withdraw, and times you want to be around people. There are times that being alone and not getting out of bed for days at a time is increasing depression. In those cases, I recommend that people speak with someone.

2. Take away the judgment that can come with grief. There is no right or wrong way to grieve.

3. Ask for what you need (if you can), verbally or nonverbally. Set boundaries around your time, space, and what information you share with people. It is ok to decide not to share aspects of the loss with people. If people ask, you can say "Can we talk about something else", "I'm not sharing that right now", or "Please respect my boundary, I'm not in a space to talk about it right now".

4. Get rid of a timeline for grief. Everyone grieves differently and for a different amount of time. Grief does not completely go away it just feels big at times or small at other times (adapted from the ball in a box grief metaphor).

5. If you have negative thoughts, extreme guilt, or if the grief begins to impact your ability to complete tasks —therapy can be helpful.

6. Use healthy coping strategies and try to avoid using unhealthy coping strategies when possible while you are actively grieving.

7. Accept support from family, friends, and your community. Some people find support groups helpful and other people find them triggering.

Special Note Some people do not feel significant emotional distress or any distress after a loss due to not having a good relationship with the individual, not being close to them, or (insert own reason).

Tips for Helping People Who are Grieving

1. Be mindful of what you say to them. Many statements that are meant to be supportive are very invalidating.

2. The power of silence. As a listener/supporter you do not need to know what to say. Sometimes one of the best things you can do for a person is sit with them in their pain and give them safe space to let it out. Please know that sitting with people in their pain is extremely uncomfortable and you will need to manage your own emotions as you listen. You may also be grieving the person as well and supporting one another can be helpful. If you are normally viewed as the helper in your family, reminding them that you are grieving too can sometimes be helpful. It is ok to show this emotion in safe spaces.

3. Let them cry. It is my recommendation to not offer tissues until they ask for it. As a therapist, we are trained that giving tissue can communicate that you want the person's tears to stop. Seeing someone you care about cry can be emotional. Remind yourself that this is good for them, and it is good for them to let it out.

4. Listen to them from their perspective and not your own. Do not compare pain unless they bring it up first. Often we try an emotional shortcut where we attempt to apply the same situation to our own lives and think about how we would feel. If this helps you have empathy, that is great. If you think you would handle the situation differently, please keep that to yourself. Unless they ask about how you have handled a loss in the past, immediately following a loss bringing up your own loss can take the focus off the griever and place it on you.

5. Do not force them to try to find the good. They will find it when they are ready or will seek support finding it.

6. If you have concerns about their safety due to them making vague comments about not knowing if they want to go on or be here, encourage them to get into therapy ASAP. Ask them if they are having unsafe thoughts and follow up with a crisis hotline, emergency services (if needed/severe), or scheduling a therapy appointment ASAP.

7. Ask them if they would like to talk about something else, go for a walk, just sit and talk, or…whatever. This can help give them permission to not talk if they do not want to at this moment.

8. Listening to them may bring up your old wounds. Manage your emotions because sitting with people in their own pain/grief can be very uncomfortable, if they begin to cry comfort them. My favorite tool to use is my breath. Taking short slow breaths when someone is expressing a lot of emotions helps me stay grounded.

Here is a chart that has some examples of what not to say, what to say, and what to do.

WHAT NOT TO SAY…	WHAT TO SAY…	WHAT TO DO…
Everything happens for a reason.	NOTHING… silence really is golden	Sit with them and comfort them.
They are in a better place.	I'm here for you if you ever want to talk.	Call/text them and offer to meet up with them.
Time heals all wounds.	I don't know what to say.	Offer to help with any household chores.
Weren't they sick/ill?	I'm here to listen if you want to share how this is impacting you.	Sit with them and just listen.
At least they lived a long life.	I'm here to listen if you ever want to share any memories or pictures.	Check in on them about 4-6 months after the loss. Often people are bombarded with support immediately following the loss.
You are young and can have another _____ (child/pet).	I can't imagine what you are going through.	Offer to go for a walk or do an outside activity with them.
At least you still have (child/pet).	If they express that they are having difficulty, validate and affirm that you see their pain and are there for them.	Offer to do a fun activity with them once they are ready.

These are my recommendations and not an exhaustive list. The key point to take away from this list is to make sure that we are giving the support that the griever needs and not saying or doing something to minimize our discomfort in a situation. If you are grieving as well, that is where silence and mutual comfort can be helpful. I will never forget going to support my family and just sitting with them with very little to say. Other family members asked what they could do to help, knowing that I am a psychologist. And all I could say is "let them grieve, let them feel this so it does not come back up later".

Avoiding Toxic Positivity

Within the past 5 years, I started hearing about 'toxic positivity' and I was immediately reminded of how I did not feel that we truly gave people space to grieve. After a few months of active grief, there are people that struggle to understand why an individual is not "back to normal". Toxic positivity is the idea that we must have a positive attitude all the time and find the bright side. Toxic positivity can deny, minimize, and invalidate the griever's emotional experiences.

I do want to acknowledge that many of the people who engage in toxic positivity have good intentions. We have put negative thinking on the 'bad' side and positive thinking on the 'good side', when the truth is that both are needed. Sitting with someone in their pain can be extremely uncomfortable. I am not recommending that you become a therapist for your friends or try to take on their emotions or grief. Counselors/therapists are trained to acknowledge, reflect, and support people in their pain. Toxic positivity says to stop feeling and just 'get over it', which can feel very invalidating for someone's experience. Also avoiding an emotion can just make it even bigger in the future.

Giving the griever and the supporter a space to be authentic can be helpful. That helps take the pressure off the supporter. You do not have to do or say anything, just give your presence and hold space for their pain. Give the griever time and give yourself time if you are the one grieving. We live in a microwave society that wants everything fast. Grief and loss are heavy tasks that are not resolved quickly. The faster you try to push through grief, in my experience, the worse it gets.

Toxic Positivity in Religious Communities/Church

There are some messages that we receive within religious communities and churches that often are not consistent with the religious text and sometimes are not the heart of the messenger. Toxic positivity is when someone is meaning to be encouraging; however, they are making statements and/or have beliefs that are harmful.

Many times, people believe that if they trust God and are 'good' then they will not experience negative emotions or go through difficult times. You can trust God AND go to therapy. Trust God AND take medication. It takes faith and courage to go to therapy and seek support. Many of the Christians that I meet within my office feel as though they are failing spiritually when they are unable to manage their depression or anxiety without therapy. I normalize this thought and encourage them to challenge it. I also encourage them to look in their Bible about the way that emotions are freely expressed.

There are many churches and pastors that are major advocates for mental health awareness within the church. They are also very supportive of people seeking therapy and support. For some people, they are not sure if they are experiencing a spiritual or a mental health issue. Honestly, sometimes these issues can be very complex and nuanced. As a therapist, if a client thinks their depression is a spiritual issue and yet they were doing well emotionally before discontinuing their medication, I encourage them to talk about their concerns with their medical doctor. I also sometimes make a little comment 'as far as I know, the devil does not respond to medication'.

You are not weak, less faithful, or less spiritual if medication helps to manage your mental health. Many of the pastors that make negative comments about mental health do not have the same beliefs about physical health. If someone has type 1 diabetes, monitoring their insulin, attending regular doctor's appointments, and taking insulin is not a lack of faith. Often we take better care of our cars, getting regular maintenance every 3,000-5,000 miles and yet we do not take care of our mental health. The things that you ignore and do not take care of, can impact you in the future.

Here are some general recommendations to create emotionally safe religious communities:

1. Be careful about the words used and how mental health is referred to in sermons.

2. Have a culture that encourages people to seek professional help when needed.

3. Provide spiritual support as requested.

4. If you are not sure what a person's needs are and you would like to pray for them, you can ask them what they would like prayer for. That can help them to feel that people are interested in them as a person and care about what they need. Hearing their need may also help people be able to address the need.

5. Have a list of licensed therapists that you can consult with and refer to if needed.

6. Be genuine and try not to make dismissive statements. Increase your ability to sit with people in difficult emotions.

Spiritual Abuse

It is important to note that people can experience spiritual abuse within their religious community. I have a YouTube video that explains this for mental health clinicians and have resources linked below. Here are a few different examples:

- Religious text being used to shame, harm, and/or and manipulate
- Authority of spiritual leader used to take advantage of others
- Coerced to give money or time

Conclusion

Grief can bring up a lot of emotions including guilt and shame. There are times that we need to look at forgiving ourselves, the other person, or God. In the next chapter, forgiveness will be defined. It is important to note what forgiveness is and what it is not. It will also cover some basic steps we can take to begin this healing journey.

RESOURCES

- *It's OK That You're Not OK: Meeting Grief and Loss in a Culture That Doesn't Understand* by Megan Devine
- *Ambiguous Loss: Learning to Live with Unresolved Grief* by Pauline Boss PhD,
- *Grieving While Black: An Antiracist Take on Oppression and Sorrow* by Breeshia Wade
- *I Wasn't Ready to Say Goodbye: Surviving, Coping, and Healing After the Sudden Death of a Loved One* by Ellen Archer, Brook Noel, et al.

- *Finding Meaning: The Sixth Stage of Grief* by David Kessler
- *Moving Through Grief: Proven Techniques for Finding Your Way After Any Loss* by Gretchen Kubacky, PsyD
- *The Grief Recovery Handbook, 20th Anniversary Expanded Edition: the Action Program for Moving Beyond Death, Divorce, and Other Losses Including Health, Career, and Faith* by John W. James, Russell Friedman, et al.
- *At a Loss: Finding Your Way After Miscarriage, Stillbirth, or Infant Death* by Donna Rothert
- *Empty Arms: Coping With Miscarriage, Stillbirth and Infant Death* by Sherokee Ilse
- *From Mourning To Knight* by Damon Silas
- *Faith That Hurts, Faith That Heals/Understanding the Fine Line Between Healthy Faith and Spiritual Abuse* by Jack Arterburn, Stephen; Felton
- *The Subtle Power of Spiritual Abuse: Recognizing and Escaping Spiritual Manipulation and False Spiritual Authority Within the Church* by David Johnson and Jeff VanVonderen
- *When Narcissism Comes to Church: Healing Your Community From Emotional and Spiritual Abuse* by Chuck DeGroat and Richard J. Mouw
- *God Can't: How to Believe in God and Love after Tragedy, Abuse, and Other Evils* by Thomas Jay Oord
- *Escaping the Maze of Spiritual Abuse: Creating Healthy Christian Cultures* by Lisa Oakley and Justin Humphreys
- *Healing Spiritual Abuse: How to Break Free from Bad Church Experience* by Ken Blue
- *Broken Trust: …a practical guide to identify and recover from toxic faith, toxic church, and spiritual abuse (The Overcoming Series: Spiritual Abuse, Book 4)* by F. Remy Diederich

CHAPTER 10

FORGIVENESS

Forgiveness has played and continues to play an important role in my life, so I would like to share some of the things I have learned along the way. Going through a process to forgive myself, others, and God helped me to live a happier and healthier life. Unforgiveness negatively impacted my view of myself and others. It also spread and had a ripple effect on people that were not even involved with the original offense. In my life, unforgiveness towards men negatively impacted my other relationships. Addressing my thoughts and feelings and getting healing for my old wound helped me have better relationships with the men around me. Often when people say they are against forgiveness, they are actually against reconciliation. Let me clarify what forgiveness is NOT; it is not forgetting, excusing, lack of justice, or reconciliation. When you forgive someone, you still remember what happened, it does not excuse their behavior, and you can still seek justice. Forgiveness is not rebuilding trust. I can forgive someone and decide that I am unable to trust them. Forgiveness is not being weak or letting the other person win. The most important point is that you can forgive someone and never speak to or see them again. There are times that people have to cut someone out of their lives completely due to safety (Enright, Freedman, & Rique, 1998).

Now that we have cleared that up, let's talk about what forgiveness IS; forgiveness is a process of letting go of the offense to free yourself. Marianne Williamson said it best, "Unforgiveness is like drinking poison yourself and waiting for the other person to die." It builds up inside of you and holds you back while the other person typically moves on with their life, barring any legal consequences for their actions. And even if there are legal consequences, you can never erase the offense. It happened and it was wrong. Continuing to carry it will only weigh you down and negatively impact your emotions, behavior, thinking, and future relationships. It can also be difficult when the person we are mad at is ourselves, God, the universe, or someone who has died. My dissertation was on forgiveness in aggressive children and showed that learning about forgiveness could reduce vengefulness in kids (Turner, 2009 my other relationships). Vengefulness is the need to seek revenge or inflict pain on the other person after an offense. Forgiveness is a gift that you give yourself, to free yourself emotionally from the individual and regain your control.

Forgiveness starts with the decision to forgive and the process that typically takes longer and is a journey is emotional forgiveness (Worthington et al., 2007). It is unconditional and is freely given as a gift with no expectation of receiving anything in return. This was a gift that I was able to give myself to free myself emotionally and spiritually. If I had said, I will forgive them when they apologize or I will forgive them when they change their behavior, I would still be waiting on them. Forgiveness gives you the power to move forward without expecting them to change. Reconciliation is about restoring trust and establishing boundaries and this option is not appropriate for every situation.

My own therapy helped me to acknowledge my hurt and work towards forgiveness of myself and others. I had tried to "let it go" on my own, prayed about it, and did not realize how much self-blame, guilt, and shame I was carrying. My breakthrough occurred when I received validation from my therapist, a complete stranger, that it was not my fault, and I did not do anything wrong. I knew those words in my head, it was freeing to hear them. A family member could have told me that and I would have likely brushed it off because they are "supposed" to say that. Hearing it from my therapist helped me accept in my heart what I already knew in my head. Forgiveness is about being able to move through the emotions, behaviors, or thoughts related to the offense. I specifically did not say 'move on' because that wording can invalidate the experience of others and make people feel that they are 'falling short'. Let's also distinguish between the decision to forgive and the emotional aspect of forgiveness. Typically, it is easy to make the decision to forgive and mentally decide to let go of the pain of the hurt. The difficulty lies in letting go of the emotions that we have carried related to the offense(s). (Worthington et al., 2007). Forgiveness is about you, moving forward without the weight of bitterness, shame, etc.

How to Forgive?

Once someone has made the decision to go on a journey towards forgiveness and take back control of their thoughts, behaviors, and emotions, the first step is to acknowledge the hurt. Identify what happened and assess the impact it had and continues to have on you. Eventually, you begin the journey to move through the pain. Unforgiveness and bitterness can blind us to our own negative behaviors and the good things in our life. We can get so focused on the other person that we do not see how we may be impacted by the people around us. The things that are revealed can be healed. Each person's journey will be unique, and I have some resources linked if people would like additional models or resources for this phase. Practice self-compassion and extend forgiveness to yourself too. Lastly, set healthy boundaries. Sometimes after an offense people go to extremes and say, 'I'm never telling anyone anything ever again.' They generalize their experience with one person and apply it to everyone. There are also people who have had multiple negative experiences with a lot of different people, therefore building trust can be extremely difficult. Emotional, physical, time, and money boundaries can be extraordinarily useful(refer back to Chapter 5 for more information). After an offense, some people shut down like a fortress and keep everything out or they have weak boundaries and let everything and anything into their lives.

1. **Decide**: to begin the process of forgiving

2. **Acknowledge:** the hurt, the emotions, and validate the right to be in pain

3. **Assess:** how these feelings are impacting you and see this is getting in your way

4. **Begin:** start the journey to move through the pain

5. **Support**: check out additional resources linked below and seek therapy or spiritual counseling/guidance if needed

6. **Self-Compassion**: more information about self-forgiveness below

7. **Boundaries:** create physical and emotional safety for yourself with appropriate boundaries that are not too rigid or too flexible

Activities that Promote Forgiveness

Here are some activities that you can try (consult a therapist if in therapy or discontinue and check out resources in Chapter 12 if distressing):

1. Journaling, poetry, song lyrics (if traumatic may need to do this with a therapist, or within the safe space of therapy)

2. Breathing techniques; breathe in peace and blow out shame, bitterness, hate, etc.

3. Put offense in a balloon and pop it

4. Write offense and safely destroy

5. Art

6. Movement (dance, exercise, etc.)

Self-Forgiveness

There are people that hold themselves to a higher standard than others. If someone else made the same mistake, they would say it was not a big deal. Yet, when they make an error, they internalize it as being a failure. Not that they made a mistake, that they are a mistake. Self-forgiveness is a gift that we give ourselves and follow many of the same steps listed above. The additional aspects that must be added are changing your behavior and making restitution and/or amends. Be mindful of your default thoughts about yourself and see if they are always negative, especially when you make a minor mistake. Often we internalize the voice of others, so be mindful about who you have around you. Are there people in your past or present that said or did things to make you feel small or insignificant? The default thoughts that you have about yourself are likely being influenced by these individuals. Practicing affirmations or "if-firmations" (discussed in Chapter 3) daily may help to challenge negative thoughts. Let go of perfectionism and allow yourself to make mistakes. You may even practice coloring outside of the lines, skipping a step in a receipt, and increasing your tolerance for mistakes. For those individuals in treatment or seeking treatment, it is important to discuss your thoughts and feelings about yourself and address the roots of your negative thoughts and emotions about yourself.

Managing Conflict

Not all conflict is bad. Usually, people that avoid conflict did not have a healthy example of conflict resolution growing up. Conflict handled appropriately can deepen relationships and help them grow after a misunderstanding. Here are some basic tips that I use with my clients to help them better manage conflicts with loved ones:

1. Remember that you are on the same team. Especially with family and friends, we can get so passionate about defending our views, ideas, or what we want, that the other person is viewed as the enemy.

2. Set ground rules around resolving conflicts with others. Here are some example ground rules: no yelling, no cursing, no name-calling, no empty threats, no shaming, use "I statements", the person who requests a 'time out' is the one who comes back to the conversation before the end of the night, listen to understand and not respond, and no bringing outside people into the conversation without the other person's approval.

3. Agree to disagree and compromise. The same person should not always be the one doing the compromising.

4. Have difficult conversations before making lifelong commitments if possible. Far too often people avoid difficult conversations, thinking that the person will change.

5. Remember that 'You do not have to attend every argument you are invited to!' Sometimes it is best to disengage and walk away to calm before saying or doing something that will harm the other person. Remember, we are on the same team. Hurting them hurts me. We cannot take back our words and they have a lasting impact on a person. I like the

saying that people will not always remember what you did but they will remember how you made them feel.

6. Give them the benefit of the doubt and challenge your internal narrative about a situation. Brené Brown talks about challenging the 'story' you are telling yourself. The example that I love to give is when I first married my husband, he would go and get food for himself and come back with food. He is not a selfish person, loves me, and cares about me and my well-being. When I was calm, I let him know that this bothered me, and he immediately understood my perspective. He also shared his perspective which I understood (I would get home from work after him, and he did not want the food to be cold). We also agreed that if he messaged me about getting food and I did not see it, that it was ok. I appreciated the attempt.

7. Remember that acceptance is not approval (DBT skill Radical Acceptance). I can accept that someone is passive-aggressive and set a boundary. If considering a long-term partnership with someone… think about this question "what if they never change?". I heard someone say you can't be mad about things that you knew before marriage in your marriage. If it was a deal-breaker, then break the deal!

Conclusion

As I mentioned earlier, my dissertation was on forgiveness in children, and I have always had a heart and a passion for them. After about 5-8 years of clinical work, I realized that I could "fix" a child over a 45-60 minute period of discussion and their parent could break them in less than a second with a single look. So, I began to shift to working more with families and helping to support families. Now being the mother of an almost 4-year-old, I really have so much more empathy for parents and enjoy supporting them. I believe that parents do the best they can, and the problems come when there is a gap between their best and the child's needs. The parent may be doing better than their abusive parents; however, they may still be causing harm to their child. Maybe it does not legally constitute abuse but is increasing depression and anxiety. I have seen this in clinical work and my own work informed my decision to not spank our child. Now, are there days when the thought crosses my mind to give a little pinch or just give a little physical reminder to follow the rules, and then I remember that while that may solve my problem in the short term, it creates long-term problems. In the next chapter, we will discuss how to teach and apply many of the skills discussed in this book to our children to raise emotionally strong and confident kids.

RESOURCES

- *Forgiveness is a Choice: A Step-by-Step Process for Resolving Anger and Restoring Hope: Enright PhD, Dr. Robert D.*
- *The Book of Forgiving: The Fourfold Path for Healing Ourselves and Our World* by Desmond Tutu, Mpho Tutu
- *Moving Forward: Six Steps to Forgiving Yourself and Breaking Free from the Past* by Everett Worthington Jr.

REFERENCES

Enright, R. D., Freedman, S., & Rique, J. (1998). The psychology of interpersonal forgiveness. In R. D. Enright & J. North (Eds.), *Exploring forgiveness* (pp. 46–62). University of Wisconsin Press.

Merril, M.. (2015, May 7). *Forgiveness: It's Not What You Think - Mark Merrill's Blog.* www.markmerrill.com/forgiveness-its-not-what-you-think

Turner, P. J. (2009). *Impact of PATTS group intervention on forgiveness in children.* Regent University.

Worthington, E. L., Witvliet, C. V. O., Pietrini, P., & Miller, A. J. (2007). Forgiveness, Health, and Well-Being: A Review of Evidence for Emotional Versus Decisional Forgiveness, Dispositional Forgivingness, and Reduced Unforgiveness. *Journal of Behavioral Medicine, 30*(4), 291–302. https://doi.org/10.1007/s10865-007-9105-8

Worthington, E. (2014). *Everett Worthington.* http://www.evworthington-forgiveness.com/reach-forgiveness-of-others

CHAPTER 11

RAISING RESILIENT CHILDREN

"Shame, blame, disrespect, betrayal, and the withholding of affection damage the roots from which love grows. Love can only survive these injuries if they are acknowledged, healed and rare."

— Brené Brown, **The Gifts of Imperfection**

Many of the same things that build resilience in adults also build resilience in children. Building things like optimism, self-esteem, self-control, flexibility, adaptability, problem-solving, emotional awareness, social support, and a sense of humor make our kids stronger, more well-rounded, and more resilient.

Develop a Growth Mindset within Your Kids

Let your kids explore and be courageous. Sometimes as parents we set limits on our children out of our own anxiety. Try not to tell your child what they cannot be or what they cannot accomplish. If they have a big dream or goal, sit down with them and talk about the steps to get there. If they end up changing their minds due to the level of effort or work that the desired goal will take, do not say 'I told you so' or 'I knew you would quit'. If they signed up for baseball, I would have them finish the season and change to a different sport next year if they desired. As a teen, I thought I wanted to be a cosmetologist and my mother was very supportive of that goal. She did let me know that I would likely need to own a chain of salons due to the amount of money I like to spend or be a celebrity hairstylist. I took cosmetology in 9th grade and realized that I like getting my hair done more than doing other people's hair. She supported my decision to shift back to wanting to be a therapist in the future. Give your child a voice and value their opinion. This does not mean that they get their way. I can value and hear that my child wants to watch five hours of television every day and also set a boundary around tv time.

Positive Parenting

There is a lot of debate on old school versus new school parenting techniques and the damage that cohesive and punitive parenting strategies can cause versus people worrying about children being coddled. My responses to anyone who says that they were spanked as a child and turned out just "fine":

1. What if your parents could have taught the same lesson and received the same result without using physical punishment, would that have been helpful for you?

2. Is there anyone else that can corroborate this "fine" you speak of?

3. Do you have difficulty managing your anger (fight), do you avoid conflict (flight), do you zone out during conflict (freeze), or are you a people pleaser (fawn)?,

Discipline should be taught, and it is difficult to teach my child that their body is their own and no one should ever touch them in a way that makes them uncomfortable, and then tell them that it is ok for me to hit them because I am their parent.

I became a therapist because somebody probably went to the school counselor and told them that my mom would threaten me. I thought it was funny and never really feared for my life. Looking back, we both agree that her comments went too far and were likely born out of how she was raised. Well, my mother's name is Johnnie and I think the counselor thought that Johnnie was my dad. The counselor did not know that my father was in Turkey, (my mom and I were living in Germany), and my mom was in the United States for a business trip. The counselor asked me difficult questions without building rapport or showing me that she cared about what I had to say or what I thought. This was how I felt based on the interaction. At that moment I realized that I could do her job at 12 or 13 years old better than her. I realized that I did not want to be an accountant like I thought, I wanted to become a counselor.

When people hear positive parenting strategies or techniques, there are people that believe that the approach is permissive. There are three main parenting styles. Authoritarian is described as high control and low warmth, authoritative is high control and high warmth, and permissive is low control and high love (Baumrind, 1967). Positive parenting techniques set consistent boundaries and expectations. The approach also adds age and developmentally appropriate expectations. There are people who are authoritarian who do not believe that children should ever cry or have a tantrum or that you correct physical aggression with physical discipline. I will never forget being at the mall one time and seeing a mother with two young children. She was trying to teach her 3-year-old not to hit his one-year-old sister. So, she popped him on the hand and said, 'don't hit'. He looked at her and popped her on the hand and said, 'don't hit'. The message was lost in the delivery. Authoritarian parenting can increase behavior problems, reduce intelligence, and cause emotional and social problems in the future (Williams et al, 2009). If physical discipline changes behavior in the moment, it is typically temporary and an attempt to avoid harm. The child typically does not learn how to problem-solve or regulate their emotions or behavior. As a psychologist, I have also seen where people were using physical discipline without knowing that there was an untreated Attention Deficit Hyperactivity Disorder (ADHD), anxiety, or depression diagnosis. Children show their emotions through their behavior.

Authoritative parenting is not allowing your child to run all over you and do whatever they feel like doing. There are still limits and boundaries. I will be honest that there are times that the thought of using old school strategies crosses my mind because new school techniques can take longer to see results. Also, the child does not have that "fear" of the parent. I do not believe that discipline of children should be predicated on them trying to not upset the adults. Discipline also should teach and not hurt or cause harm.

Here is an example of a positive parenting technique I like to use. During a corrective moment with a child, use Dr. Bruce Perry's three R's: Regulate, Relate, and Reason. This is an approach that first focuses on calming the child, connecting with them, and correcting the behavior. Dr. Bruce Perry also talks about the four S's that children need to develop a secure attachment: Seen, Safe, Soothed, and Secure. Additional tools and recommendations will be provided later in this chapter.

There are so many support tools and resources available to me as a parent that my mother did not have. There are a lot of things that worked in past generations that just are not working now. There has been an increase in emotional issues in children and often when there is something wrong kids show that through their behaviors before they will use their language. Even with teenagers, you sometimes see it in their attitude and behavior before they tell you what's really going on with them.

What's Wrong with These Kids?

I use humor a lot with the families that I support, and we talk about the fact that the old school way doesn't work for these kids now. I was parented in a way where respect was demanded. My mom did respect me, and she also gave me a voice. We all know that the parenting tools my grandmother and great-grandmother used are now legally considered physical abuse. On the Adverse Childhood Experiences Scale (ACEs) the first question is about whether or not your parents ever insult or humiliate you, or act in a way that makes you fear for your physical safety. The second question is about the use of physical discipline.

Old school techniques are currently creating more harm than good right now. Yelling, shaming, blaming, and physical discipline have an impact on the developing brain. What is the major difference between when I was parented and this current generation? I joke with families and blame Google and social media. I honestly believe that kids are appropriately being taught about consent and desire mutual respect. It is illegal for me to hit my husband, but in the state of Virginia, it is not illegal for me to spank my child within limits. I choose to use strategies that teach and do not cause harm. Here are some basic tips for parents to take a gentler approach with their children:

1. **Model the behavior that you want to see.** The days of telling kids to do what you say and not what you do is over. That strategy seemed to work in the past, and I can promise you that it does not work for a majority of kids now. Children are mirrors of ourselves and show us things that we have to work on. In my clinical work I like to explain to parents that they have a fully developed brain and in order for change to happen, they have to model the behaviors that they want.

2. **Validate emotions, not behavior.** If my child is having a tantrum because he did not get his way. I can validate that it is frustrating to not get your way and help him accept no as an answer.

3. **Determine your child's skills deficits**. There is a difference between thinking my child is lazy and helping them address a lack of motivation and drive. If your child struggles with managing their emotions, practicing things that help to regulate emotion when the child is calm can be helpful. With young children, this may be blowing bubbles to practice letting things go and/or breathing techniques. With older children, I enjoy using competitive games to teach emotion regulation and problem-solving skills.

4. **Determine your child's strengths.** Identify your child's strengths and try to catch them doing good and using those skills.

5. **Reframe your thinking about behavior and do not take it personally.** If it feels like your child is intentionally trying to ruin your day and 'make' you mad, then learn to not give them a response. Regulating your emotions ends that behavior, even if you have to fake it at first and own your emotional triggers. Often behaviors that are very triggering are rooted in my own history and how I was raised. If your child is engaging in a behavior like this, it may be helpful to partner with a therapist. Instead of thinking your child is manipulative, remove opportunities for them to manipulate by using communication and practicing the next tip.

6. **Be clear, concise, and consistent.** Boundaries and consistency help to stop manipulation. Children will do what works and most children will eventually stop behavior that does not work. If your child is having an "attitude", ask them to change their tone of voice. Do not set a consequence out of your own emotion. Regulate your emotions first, connect, and then correct the behavior.

7. **Give your kid a redo and be playful for minor situations.** For example, if your child comes up and says something in an inappropriate tone, ask them to rewind and try again. You may even be able to laugh about this with your child if they are not too upset. When people are upset they are more likely to see feedback as criticism.

8. **Remember the Whole Brain Approach.** Check out this technique developed by Dan Siegel.

9. **Reduce opportunities to lie by not asking questions that you know the answer to.** If you know that your child broke something then talk about it. They may deny it and you can talk about how you know or say that you are not going to argue about it. With online learning, I encourage parents to check grades routinely (at least weekly). It is really easy for students to fall behind due to the high number of assignments due regularly.

10. **Model that it is ok to make mistakes.** Admit and apologize when you are wrong. Everyone needs to learn this skill.

It is Never Too Late to Shift

If you are reading this and realizing that you would like to make some changes with your teenage or adult children, know that it is never too late to make adjustments. It is important that we listen to and connect with our children before we correct them. I recently heard someone say that once children are 13-14 years old our role as a parent changes to more of a guide. It is our role as a parent to prepare our children with the tools that they need to succeed in the world. This will look different for each child and every child has a different level of independence that they are able to achieve. Here are some tips for older children:

1. Give your child a voice

2. Respect their voice AND set boundaries

3. Teach them how to disagree appropriately

4. Teach your child how to advocate for themselves and take responsibility for their actions

5. Teach them how to problem-solve

6. If your child is having major issues, please reach out for help

Special note for Black parents and/or parents of Black children

As the mother of a Black son, I would be lying if I said that I do not worry about his safety in our world. Even with that fear, I can show him how the world should be in our home. The world is not fair, and he has to comply with no questions in the real world. I strongly believe that I can teach my son these things based on the experiences that he has in our neighborhood, in stores, in school and that we can create safety within our home. We can create a space where he is able to ask questions, disagree appropriately, and attempt to problem-solve. He will also have to accept no as an answer and respect self, others, and property.

Finding Purpose Outside of Parent Role

It is important to have identity and purpose outside of being a parent. You are still a person with your own wants and desires. After having my first and only child, the next two to three years I had to rediscover myself as a woman, wife, mother, friend, and businesswoman. Self-care and having your own dreams and desires is not inherently selfish. There are ways to engage in these tasks that leave you refreshed and ready to support your family even more. You cannot give what you do not have. It is not on your children or partner to fill those spaces within your life.

There are people who try to live their lives through their children and have difficulty letting them become who they were created to be. I remember when I told my Mom that I wanted to be a psychologist after wanting to be an accountant just like her. She did not let me know her disappointment and managed her emotions on her own. No matter what goal I talked with her about, she never told me that it was too much. Instead, she would discuss the things I would need to do and invest to reach that goal. The purpose and goals that you have today can grow and change as you do the same. Similarly, your children may also do the same. Individuals born after 1985 are more likely to have multiple jobs and change jobs every 2-3 years due to changing work requirements and fewer jobs offering paid pensions/incentives for staying with them for 20 plus years (Adkins, 2016).

Your history can help you tap into your destiny. Your current situation does not have to define you or your family. Identifying your individual and family goals can help you shift your perspective, emotions, and behavior. When I view my time as an investment into my child's future, watching his favorite YouTube episode for the 80th time does not feel as bad. Also taking time to intentionally invest time and energy into what you want as well. Some people struggle with thinking about and doing for themselves. So, it is ok to start small.

Questions that Can Help You on this Journey:

1. Who am I?
2. What do I want?
3. What do I enjoy?
4. Where would I like to see myself in the next year?
5. How does pouring into myself benefit my family?

Parent-Shaming

The person with the 'best' parenting advice and the one who has it all together, is someone who does not have any kids. I'm saying this jokingly and honestly, having my own child gave me so much empathy for parents. There were things that I did not understand until I had my child. It is great that there is so much information available online about parenting, but it can be a daunting task to wade through all the information and come out with what you need.

As a psychologist and a person who loves to get information and research, I had to accept that my child does not fit neatly into any one book. It is really important, as you are making decisions to raise resilient children, that you do not compare yourself to others. It can be really difficult when you are trying to coach your child through a tantrum, and it feels as though everyone is judging you. Your child may have more or less difficulties right now than a friend's child. Finding a group of supportive parents that will be honest with you about what is and is not working for them can be key during difficult times. Also, remembering that the seeds you are planting now may not see results for years down the road.

Different does not mean better. If you have a family member or friend that is trying different techniques, those may not work for you. Make sure to do what works best for you and your family. Also, be prepared to shift when needed. Recently, we had to start to teach lessons on respect and set more boundaries with our son at home due to difficulties he was having at daycare. No one will ever be happy with all of your decisions, but you should be confident in them.

Finding help and support for your child can be incredibly difficult and confusing. I have compiled some of the questions I am frequently asked here. If you have concerns about your child, please do not ignore them. There has been a rise in death by suicide in children of all races and ethnic groups. It is currently the second leading cause of death in individuals 10-34 years old (NIMH» Suicide, 2021).

Signs Your Child May Need Help

- Developmental delays

- Excess energy/difficulty sitting still

- Extreme moodiness

- Talking and/or thinking about harming self or others
- Change in academic performance
- Withdrawal from friends
- Change in behaviors
- Learning difficulty (taking an excessive amount of time to complete work… do not assume it is an effort issue)

Steps to Seek Support (in no particular order)

1. Do not be afraid to seek support and ask questions.
2. Discuss concerns with the school, pediatrician, and or therapist/counselor.
3. Request a psychological evaluation if recommended by the school, pediatrician, or therapist or you have major concerns about your child. It can often take 2-6 months to schedule an evaluation, so starting with therapy can often be helpful. The therapist can also provide the psychologist with their observations for the evaluation as well.
4. Remember that children communicate with their behaviors first. Set boundaries and have natural consequences. Encourage your child/children and try to catch them 'doing good'.
5. If your child is in crisis, contact emergency services and head to the emergency room or your medical doctor for a mental health screening. If your child is under the age of 18 years old and there are concerns about their ability to remain safe within the home, the following options will likely be explored:

1. The medical team will ask if your child will agree to be safe, develop a safety plan, and schedule follow-up outpatient appointments with a counselor and/or psychiatrist.

2. The medical team will recommend a brief psychiatric hospitalization. For children, it is typically 2-14 days. As the parent, you can discuss concerns with this option if you are not on board. In the USA, psychiatric hospitalization is often best when there is believed to be an imminent safety concern and adjusting medications under 24-hour supervision is necessary.

3. If the concern is chronic and there have been multiple brief/acute psychiatric hospitalizations, the team may recommend residential placement (out of home treatment for approximately 6-12 months depending on the program). In my experience, this should be the last resort because an out-of-home placement can increase feelings of rejection and abandonment in your child. Never threaten psychiatric treatment as a punishment. These options should only be considered for imminent safety concerns. Some children thrive in out-of-home placements due to the structure, attention, and support available. There also may be some dynamics within the home that family therapy would be helpful to address.

Important Terms to Know (additional terms in Chapter 12): *this information applies to the USA*

- <u>Child Study:</u> a meeting to determine if a child qualifies for educational accommodations based on learning difficulties or a medical diagnosis.

- Individualized Education Plan (IEP): legal accommodations through special education. There is often funding associated with IEP accommodations.

- 504 Plan: legal accommodations to accommodate a learning difficulty or medical diagnosis that does not meet the criteria for an IEP.

- Psychologist: a mental health professional that can complete psychological testing. Many psychologists also provide therapy.

- Psychiatrist: a medical doctor that specializes in treating mental health diagnoses. You can request an appointment with a psychiatrist to discuss options. The decision to medication is a parental decision and discussing options, concerns, and benefits with a medical doctor can be helpful.

- School Psychologist: a school official that is typically present at Child Study and IEP meetings. If approved by the school, the school psychologist can do educational testing.

- School Social Worker: school official that provides school-based therapy and can help when families need support or resources.

- School Guidance Counselor: provides mental health support to students within schools within their level of training and expertise. Some schools have licensed social workers or counselors that are available to meet with students in crisis or with significant mental health needs.

Tips for Seeking Support

- **Academic/School Concerns:** If concerned about your child's academic performance (in the USA), request a Child

Study. Schools are required by law to provide a child study meeting within a certain time. If your child has an Individualized Education Plan or a 504 Plan.

- **Emotional/Behavioral Concerns**: Vulnerability is one of the best things we can do for our children and seek out resources and support WHEN we need it. No parent is perfect, and we all can use a helping hand. As a licensed psychologist that specializes in working with children and teens, my therapy has been and will continue to be one of the best things that I do for my family. At times we can repeat negative patterns from the past or do "better" than the previous generation and still not meet the needs of our child/children. The next chapter has a variety of resources and tools to support you along your journey.

RESOURCES

- *The Whole-Brain Child: 12 Revolutionary Strategies to Nurture Your Child's Developing Mind* by Daniel J. Siegel, M.D. and Tina Payne Bryson, M.D.
- *Parenting from the Inside Out: How a Deeper Self-Understanding Can Help You Raise Children Who Thrive: 10th Anniversary Edition* by Daniel J. Siegel, Mary Hartzell
- *The Conscious Parent: Transforming Ourselves, Empowering Our Children* by Dr. Shefali Tsabary
- *How to Talk So Kids Will Listen & Listen So Kids Will Talk* by Adele Faber and Elaine Mazlish
- *Peaceful Parent, Happy Siblings: How to Stop the Fighting and Raise Friends for Life* by Dr. Laura Markham
- *Parenting Apart: How Separated and Divorced Parents Can Raise Happy and Secure Kids* by Christina McGhee

- *Parenting from the Inside Out: How a Deeper Self-Understanding Can Help You Raise Children Who Thrive: 10th Anniversary Edition* by Daniel J. Siegel and Mary Hartzell
- *Raising Good Humans: A Mindful Guide to Breaking the Cycle of Reactive Parenting and Raising Kind, Confident Kids* by Hunter Clarke-Fields MSAE and Carla Naumburg PhD
- *No-Drama Discipline: the whole-brain way to calm the chaos and nurture your child's developing mind (Mindful Parenting)* by Daniel J. Siegel, Tina Payne Bryson
- *Emotional Intensity in Gifted Students: Helping Kids Cope with Explosive Feelings* by Christine Fonseca

Children's Books

- *A Little SPOT of Emotion 8 Book Box Set (Books 1-8: Anger, Anxiety, Peaceful, Happiness, Sadness, Confidence, Love, & Scribble Emotion)* by Diane Alber
- A Little SPOT Takes Action! 8 Book Box Set (Books 9-16: Kindness, Responsibility, Patience, Respect, Honesty, Organization, Diversity, & Safety) by Diane Alber
- *A Little SPOT of Empathy: A Story about Understanding and Kindness* by Diane Alber
- *Breathe Like a Bear: 30 Mindful Moments for Kids to Feel Calm and Focused Anytime, Anywhere* by Kira Willey and Anni Betts

Children's TV Shows/Movies

*Daniel Tiger's Neighborhood

*Sesame Street

*Esme and Roy

*Little Einsteins

*Stinky and Dirty

*Inside Out

*Doc McStuffins

REFERENCES

Adkins, A. (2016, May 12). . Gallup.com; Gallup. https://www.gallup.com/workplace/231587/millennials-job-hopping-generation.aspx

Baumrind, D. (1967). Effects of authoritative control on child behavior. *Child Development, 37*(4), 887–907.

Goleman, D. (1995). *Emotional intelligence: Why it can matter more than IQ.* New York: Bantam Books.

NIMH» Suicide. (2021, May 6). Nih.gov. https://www.nimh.nih.gov/health/statistics/suicide

Siegel, D. J., & Hartzell, M. (2005). *Parenting from the inside out.* Jeremy P Tarcher.

Williams, L. R., Degnan, K. A., Perez-Edgar, K. E., Henderson, H. A., Rubin, K. H., Pine, D. S., Steinberg, L., & Fox, N. A. (2009). Impact of behavioral inhibition and parenting style on internalizing and externalizing problems from early childhood through adolescence. *Journal of abnormal child psychology, 37*(8), 1063–1075. https://doi.org/10.1007/s10802-009-9331-3

CHAPTER 12

ADDITIONAL RESOURCES

Thank you for checking out these additional resources. It is my hope that this chapter will be a support to you both now and in the future. This information is for reference only and is not a specific recommendation for your situation. This chapter includes the following:

- How to find a therapist, red and green flags in therapy, and how to address conflict/questions with your therapist
- Psychologist, Psychiatrist, Social Worker, Counselor...what is the difference?
- Therapy versus Coaching
- Therapeutic approaches and treatment modalities
- Resources: trauma, parenting, emotion regulation/self-help, & Dialectical Behavior Therapy skills (DBT)
- Additional resources to check out on YouTube, Tiktok, & Podcasts

How do I find a therapist/Questions to Ask/Information?

One of the most common questions I receive on social media is "how do I find a therapist?" or I have a therapist and how do I bring ____ up with them? If you would like one website with most of this information, check out a resource developed by @my_destanation

www.mydestanation.com

special note Finding the right therapist can be a lengthy and time-consuming process. The first person that you try, may not be the right fit. You can normally tell within the first 2-3 sessions if someone is the right fit for you. Once you have made the decision to find a therapist, please persist until you have found someone. Many of the directories listed below have an option to email a potential therapist. Before you get into your story you want to ask if the person accepts insurance (if you plan to use your insurance) if they have availability, and if they work with people with _(insert one to three word description of reason seeking therapy)_.

A. Insurance or Cash Pay?

One of the first decisions people have to make is if they want to use their insurance or pay out of pocket for services. There are some therapists that do not accept insurance; however, they provide a "superbill" (a receipt with your diagnosis code and the procedure code) that you can submit for reimbursement if you have "out of network benefits". You would want to confirm with your insurance company what the rate of reimbursement will be. Also, it is important to note that some diagnoses are not covered by insurance if not deemed "medically necessary".

Free or Reduced Cost Options

- **Open Path Collective** offers individual therapy ($30-60 per hour) and couple's therapy ($80 per hour) with a licensed therapist. www.OpenPathCollective.org

- **University Counseling Center**

- **Local Community/State Funded Counseling Center**

B. Therapist Directories

Here is a list of online directories to find a therapist that meets your needs. I recommend that potential clients review the therapist's website, online profile, and any public social media (if available) to see if they may be a good fit for you. The single most important factor in therapy is the therapeutic relationship.

https://www.inclusivetherapists.com

https://www.therapyden.com

https://therapyforblackgirls.com

https://therapyforblackmen.org

www.psychologytoday.com

www.inclusivetherapists.com

www.cliniciansofcolor.org

https://therapyforqpoc.com

www.therapyforlatinx.com

www.muslimmentalhealth.com

Special note about apps that offer mental health treatment Be sure to read the privacy agreement and research to see if the treatment offered will meet your needs. Often these online apps offer an affordable rate; however, services are limited to phone and text messages. These companies also often have disclaimers that they do not provide a diagnosis and are unable to complete paperwork for legal, employment, disability, or medical reasons.

C. Common Questions to Ask During Initial Consultation/Phone Call

1. Are you a licensed therapist or currently working towards licensure? Some individuals are supervisees and are working towards obtaining their license to practice independently.
2. What approach do you use with clients?
3. How long do you typically work with clients?
4. What types of cases do you not work with or refer out to another provider?
5. Are you available outside of sessions/do you offer crisis counseling? Many therapists use hotlines for crisis calls and make themselves available for basic questions about scheduling during business hours. There are some therapists that offer crisis support at an additional fee (sometimes this is not covered by insurance, so be sure to ask if you have questions to avoid a surprise bill).

6. How do you prefer to receive feedback (in session, phone, email, etc.)?

D. Found a therapist...now what?

One of the most important factors in therapy is your relationship with the therapist. If you have an issue or would like something to be different in treatment, please bring it up with your therapist. If it is a major issue, then you may want to find someone new. I have heard some horror stories about bad experiences in therapy in my office and on Tiktok.

E. Therapist Green Flags

Signs that treatment is working, and your therapist is the right fit

   a. Feeling heard and understood
   b. Validates your feelings and challenges you to grow
   c. Accepts feedback
   d. Culturally aware

F. Therapist Red Flags

   a. Defensive and not open to feedback
   b. Relies on clients to be the sole educator on areas of difference (e.g., religion, sexual orientation, gender, race, ethnicity, etc.)
   c. Overshares about their personal life to the point where it feels like it is their therapy
   d. Not respectful of your boundaries and/or has poor boundaries

Some people are looking for therapists that are sex-positive, body-positive, LGBTQ affirming, culturally aware, etc. If this is you, please ask about the therapists' approach with __(insert population)__ clients during an initial consultation or search for therapists that specialize in treating these populations.

Therapy versus Coaching

If you are struggling with minor issues that do not meet criteria for a psychological disorder, then coaching may be a good option for you. Coaching tends to be time-limited and focuses on goal-setting, personal growth, and behavioral change. Many coaches offer a free 15 minute to 1-hour consultation to determine if they are the right fit for you. It is important to ask about their experience and training (if that is important to you) also their approach with cases like yours. I would also ask about how to terminate the agreement if coaching is not working for you.

The main differences between therapy and coaching

- Diagnosis: insurance reimbursement for a licensed therapist requires a diagnosis. Coaches do not provide diagnoses. Educational Requirements: there are minimum education and training requirements for therapists. There are no educational requirements for coaches.
- Licensing Requirements: licensed therapists have to complete steps to renew their license annually. Pastoral counselors or spiritual counselors are not always licensed. Some coaches have completed national certifications and are certified coaches. Coaches are able to provide services without a license or certification. Here is a list of the 7 Best Life Coach Certification Programs of 2021 according to an article by Amanda Capritto:
    - Best Overall: Institute for Professional Excellence in Coaching
    - Best Intensive: Institute for Life Coach Training Professional Certification
    - Best Health-Focused: Health Coach Institute Dual Life and Health Coaching Certification
    - Best for a Career Change: CoachU Core Essentials Program
    - Best for Personal Development: Life Purpose Life Coach Certification

- o Best Advanced: Integrative Wellness Academy Master Life Coaching Program
- o Best Quick: Certified Life Coach Institute Life Coach Certification

Example site to find a certified coach www.coachingfederation.org

- Continuing Education/Training: licensed therapists are required to complete a certain number of hours of continuing education annually. There are no requirements for coaches (unless related to a certification).
- Complaints/Reporting Issues: if an issue arises with a licensed therapist, clients are able to report to their local human rights advocate and the licensing board if needed.
- Ethics and boundaries: therapists are accountable to their licensing board and professionally are guided by a set of ethical principles. Coaches do not have a professional code of ethics unless provided in a certification program. Many coaches agree to not practice outside of their area of expertise and refer to licensed providers when needed.

  Examples of different types of coaches from www.flowcoachinginstitute.com/types-of-coaching/:

  - Life Coach
  - Wellness Coach
  - Relationship Coach
  - Parenting Coach
  - Youth Coach
  - Spiritual Coach
  - Financial Coach
  - Executive/Corporate Coach
  - Small Business Coach
  - Career Coach

Psychologist, Psychiatrist, Social Worker, Counselor...what is the difference?

This is a question that I frequently get when people call to make an appointment and also on social media. The information provided below is mostly based on the USA.

1. **Psychologist** is an individual who is licensed as a psychologist and able to complete psychological testing. Not every psychologist offers testing, but this is one of the biggest differences between a psychologist and a master's level therapist. Just because someone is a psychologist, does not mean that they will be a better fit for counseling. There are lots of different types of psychologists including clinical, forensic, school, and counseling.

2. **Psychiatrist** or a psychiatric nurse is an individual that is able to prescribe medication for mental health disorders. Some diagnoses can be treated by a primary care/general practice doctor.

3. **Licensed Clinical Social worker (LCSW)** is an individual with a graduate degree in Social work and is able to provide counseling. Many LCSWs are in private practice (currently Medicare only approves LCSWs or Psychologists for mental health treatment). Often people only think of Child or Adult Protective Services (CPS/APS), hospitals, or other large agencies when thinking about social workers.

4. **Licensed Counselor** (Licensed Professional Counselor-LPC, Licensed Marriage and Family Therapist-LMFT, Licensed Mental Health Counselor-LMHP) The available licenses vary based on your state/country.

5. **Lay/Spiritual Counselor** (not licensed) some religious organizations and/or church leaders offer training spiritual

counseling. This is meant for issues related to a person's faith/spirit and not a mental health diagnosis. Typically, spiritual/pastoral counselors will refer to licensed professionals if someone presents with significant mental health issues. There are licensed counselors that provide spiritual counseling and/or integrate faith into treatment when requested.

Therapy Approaches/Treatment Modalities

There are many different types of treatment. This list includes some popular treatment modalities and approaches. The therapeutic relationship you have with your counselor is more important than the specific type of treatment used. Here are some popular treatment modalities:

1. Eye Movement Desensitization and Reprocessing (EMDR) Treatment that is effective for trauma includes EMDR. Find an EMDR certified therapist https://www.emdria.org/find-a-therapist/

2. Trauma-focused cognitive behavior therapy. "Trauma-Focused Cognitive Behavioral Therapy (TF-CBT) is an evidence-based treatment for children and adolescents impacted by trauma and their parents or caregivers." https://tfcbt.org

3. Cognitive Behavior Therapy (CBT) is a very popular form of therapy that addresses how our thinking, emotions, and behaviors are connected. The goal of CBT is to change problematic thinking patterns. *Some people experience CBT as invalidating of their experience

4. Acceptance Commitment Therapy (ACT) "uses acceptance and mindfulness strategies, together with commitment and behavior change strategies, to increase psychological flexibility." (*ACT | Association for Contextual Behavioral Science*, 2021)

5. Internal Family Systems "is also known as "parts work," is a holistic, evidence-based approach to psychotherapy that identifies and addresses multiple sub-personalities or families within each person's mental system, each with its own viewpoint and qualities." (*New to Internal Family Systems (IFS)? Here are the Basics ... | PSI*, 2020)

6. Dialectical Behavior Therapy (DBT) is an approach developed by Dr. Marsha Linehan that includes individual therapy, group therapy, and crisis support. DBT uses a non-judgmental approach to teach and practice skills to address emotional reactivity, black and white/all or nothing thinking, interpersonal skills deficits, and impulsive/unsafe thoughts and/or behaviors. Some therapists use components of DBT/skills training.

7. Motivational Interviewing is a therapeutic approach that attempts to elicit change in a client's behavior by increasing intrinsic motivation.

8. Additional types of therapy that providers can get certified in (some people will use art techniques but not be a certified art therapist): Play Therapy, Art Therapy, Music therapy, Equine therapy, Sex therapy. Also, a special note that Trauma Informed Care is a system-wide approach and is not a specific form of treatment. A therapist could be trauma informed and not equipped to counsel individuals with severe trauma.

ALTERNATIVE TREATMENTS

There are lots of things that some people find therapeutic but are not considered "therapy". For example (these are for general reference):

*music	*dance	*yoga
*massage	*video games	*physical activity
*art/crafts	*time with friends	*spiritual practice

*vacation   *time in nature   *essential oils

*meditation   *cooking   *cleaning

*time with pets   *holistic treatment

*General Tip: if you are having unexplained depression, anxiety, sleep difficulty, etc., complete a physical with your medical doctor and discuss concerns to rule out a medical issue. Also, individuals with chronic pain are more likely to experience mental health issues.

TRAUMA RESOURCES

- *The Deepest Well: Healing the Long-Term Effects of Childhood Adversity* by Burke Harris M.D., Nadine
- *The Boy Who Was Raised as a Dog: And Other Stories from a Child Psychiatrist's Notebook--What Traumatized Children Can Teach Us About Loss, Love, and Healing* by Bruce D. Perry & Maia Szalavitz
- *The Body Keeps the Score: Brain, Mind, and Body in the Healing of Trauma* by Bessel van der Kolk M.D.
- *Attached: The New Science of Adult Attachment and How It Can Help You Find - and Keep – Love* by Amir Levine, Rachel Heller
- *It Didn't Start with You: How Inherited Family Trauma Shapes Who We Are and How to End the Cycle* by Mark Wolynn
- *Healing Your Past: How to overcome rejection, shame, and regret and step into your future.* by Dr. Faith Wokoma

PARENTING RESOURCES

- *The Yes Brain: How to Cultivate Courage, Curiosity, and Resilience in Your Child* by Daniel J. Siegel, Tina Payne Bryson
- *No-Drama Discipline: The Whole-Brain Way to Calm the Chaos and Nurture Your Child's Developing Mind* by Daniel J. Siegel
- *The Whole-Brain Child: 12 Revolutionary Strategies to Nurture Your Child's Developing Mind* by Daniel J. Siegel

- *Anxious Kids, Anxious Parents: 7 Ways to Stop the Worry Cycle and Raise Courageous and Independent Children* by Reid Wilson, Lynn Lyons LICSW
- Free E-Book *Playing With Anxiety (*companion book for kids and parents for *Anxious Kids, Anxious Parents)* www.playingwithanxiety.com
- *The Neurosequential Model in Education: Introduction to the NME Series: Trainer's Guide (NME Training Guide)* by Bruce D. Perry, Steve Graner

ADOPTION RESOURCES

- *The Connected Parent: Real-Life Strategies for Building Trust and Attachment* by Lisa Qualls, Dr. Karyn Purvis
- *The Connected Child: Bring hope and healing to your adoptive family* by Karyn B. Purvis, David R. Cross, Wendy Lyons Sunshine
- *20 Things Adoptive Parents Need to Succeed..Discover the Unique Need of Your Adopted Child and Become the Best Parent You Can* by Sherrie Eldridge
- *Honestly Adoption: Answers to 101 Questions About Adoption and Foster Care* by Mike Berry, Kristin Berry
- *What White Parents Should Know about Transracial Adoption: An Adoptee's Perspective on Its History, Nuances, and Practices* Melissa Guida-Richards
- *Inside Transracial Adoption* by Beth Hall, Gail Steinberg

KIDS BOOKS

- *Listening with My Heart: A story of kindness and self-compassion* by Gabi Garcia
- *The Invisible String* by Patrice Karst and Joanne Lew-Vriethoff

- *The Invisible String Workbook: Creative Activities to Comfort, Calm, and Connect* by Patrice Karst , Dana Wyss , et al.
- *I AM...: Positive Affirmations for Brown Girls* by Ayesha Rodrigue
- *I Just Don't Like the Sound of No! My Story About Accepting No for an Answer and Disagreeing the Right Way! (Best Me I Can Be)* by Julia Cook
- *Just Want to Do It My Way! My Story about Staying on Task and Asking for Help* by Julia Cook
- *But It's Not My Fault! (Responsible Me!)* by Julia Cook
- *Mistakes Are How I Learn: An Early Reader Rhyming Story Book for Children to Help with Perseverance and Diligence* by Kiara Wilson
- *I Choose to Try Again: A Colorful, Rhyming Picture Book About Perseverance and Diligence (Teacher and Therapist Toolbox: I Choose)* by Elizabeth Estrada
- *A Little SPOT of Empathy: A Story about Understanding and Kindness* by Diane Alber

DEPRESSION/ANXIETY/SELF-HELP RESOURCES

- *The Antidote: Happiness for People Who Can't Stand Positive Thinking* by Oliver Burkeman
- *10% Happier: How I Tamed the Voice in My Head, Reduced Stress Without Losing My Edge, and Found a Self-Help That Actually Works* by Dan Harris
- *Stopping the Noise in Your Head : the New Way to Overcome Anxiety and Worry* by Dr. Reid Wilson PhD
- *Marked: Understanding and Unraveling The Call Of God On Your Life* by Dr. Faith Wokoma

DBT SKILLS RESOURCES

- *DBT® Skills Training Handouts and Worksheets, Second Edition Second Edition* by Marsha Linehan
- *The Dialectical Behavior Therapy Skills Workbook (A New Harbinger Self-Help Workbook)* by Matthew McKay
- *Dialectical Behavior Therapy Skills Training with Adolescents: A Practical Workbook for Therapists, Teens & Parents* by Jean Eich
- *Stopping the Pain: A Workbook for Teens Who Cut and Self Injure* by Lawrence E. Shapiro PhD
- *The Self-Esteem Workbook for Teens: Activities to Help You Build Confidence and Achieve Your Goals* by Lisa M. Schab LCSW
- *Don't Let Your Emotions Run Your Life for Teens: Dialectical Behavior Therapy Skills for Helping You Manage Mood Swings, Control Angry Outbursts, and ... with Others (Instant Help Book for Teens) Part of: Instant Help Book for Teens (5 Books)* | by Sheri Van Dijk MSW
- *Don't Let Your Emotions Run Your Life for Kids: A DBT-Based Skills Workbook to Help Children Manage Mood Swings, Control Angry Outbursts, and Get Along with Others* by Jennifer J. Solin PsyD and Christina Kress MSW LICSW

YOUTUBE RESOURCES: Here are some of my favorite mental health channels (DrPatriceBerry):

- Kati Morton
- Psych Central
- Wellcast
- Psych2Go
- Self-Help Toons
- Micheline Maalouf
- Karyn Purvis Institute of Child Development (adoption)

TIKTOK RESOURCES: Here are a few of my favorite Tiktok Therapists, Coaches, & Psychiatrists (@drpatriceberry):

@my_destination
@thetattoedcounselor
@janellehettick
@thehappyhealer
@ask_a_therapist
@h_e_z_y_helps
@raquelmartinphd
@theshaniproject
@therapist.ashley
@thesituationaltherapist
@mattphifercoaching
@artnerdtherapy
@dr.marielbuque
@musictherapycait
@Quirky.queer.therapist
@millennialtherapy
@doctorshepardmd
@my.bald.therapy
@kendyl_mind_fulltherapy

@sassydelta
@lesleypsyd
@thepsychdoctormd
@MelissaParksSays
@that.nerdy.therapist
@ThatFatDoctor
@jessicaleighphd
@chelsey_nicole82
@leveluptherapy
@notyourtherapistdude
@thecoachingcounselor
@tiara.burns.lpcmhsp
@kimberly.anderson
@homegirltherapist
@embodimend
@latina_therapy.lcsw
@counselingforcreatives
@notyouraveragetherapist

@drhanren
@drpatpsych
@christina_lpc
@truthheals
@therapylux
@counselorwill

PODCASTS RESOURCES: (Legacy Moments)

- ❖ 10 Percent Happier
- ❖ Flusterclux with Lynn Lyons (for parents with anxious children)

Best Mental Health Podcasts of 2021 according to VeryWellMind.com (https://www.facebook.com/verywell, 2021)

- ❖ Best Overall: The Positive Psychology Podcast
- ❖ Best for Anxiety: The Anxiety Podcast
- ❖ Best for Time Constraints: Meditation Minis

- Best for Humor: The Hilarious World of Depression
- Best for Emotional Trauma: The Trauma Therapist Podcast
- Best for Complex Topics: Tara Brach

The Best Mental Health Podcasts to Take You Through the Year according to Healthline.com (Jewell, 2021)

- 'The Nod'
- 'Therapy for Black Girls'
- 'Throwing Shade'
- 'Cafeteria Christian'
- 'Mental Illness Happy Hour'
- 'WTF with Marc Maron'
- 'Code Switch'
- 'The Happiness Lab'
- '2 Dope Queens'
- 'The Hilarious World of Depression'

REFERENCES

ACT | Association for Contextual Behavioral Science. (2021). Contextualscience.org. https://contextualscience.org/act

https://www.facebook.com/verywell. (2021). *Best Mental Health Podcasts of 2021*. Verywell Mind. https://www.verywellmind.com/best-mental-health-podcasts-5097922

https://www.facebook.com/verywell. (2021). *The 7 Best Life Coach Certification Programs of 2021*. Verywell Mind. https://www.verywellmind.com/best-life-coach-certification-programs-5070205

Jewell, T. (2021, April 21). *The Best Mental Health Podcasts to Take You Through the Year*. Healthline; Healthline Media.

https://www.healthline.com/health/mental-health-podcast

Linehan MM, Schmidt HI, Dimeff LA, et al. Dialectical behavior therapy for patients with borderline personality disorder and drug-dependence. *Am J Addict.* 1999; 8:279–92.

New to Internal Family Systems (IFS)? Here are the Basics | PSI. (2020, August 6). PSI. https://psinyc.org/new-to-internal-family-systems/

ABOUT THE AUTHOR

Dr. Patrice Berry is a licensed psychologist who is passionate about providing quality mental health services to children, teens, families, and adults. She has over 15 years of experience and has worked in a variety of settings including juvenile justice, psychiatric hospitals, residential treatment, acute psychiatric treatment, community services, intensive in-home, outpatient, and school-based treatment. In April 2020, Dr. Berry opened her clinical practice, Four Rivers Psychological Services, after her full-time position ended due to schools closing. In January 2021, Dr. Berry launched her second business Mind Your Legacy, LLC to separate her clinical (therapy, psychological testing) and nonclinical services (speaking, coaching, products, and social media).

She considers herself to be a psychologist that is a Christian. Meaning that she ethically integrates faith into therapy for individuals/families that desire to include their faith as part of their treatment. She affirms, supports, and advocates for the rights of the LGBTQ+ community. As a heterosexual cisgender African American woman, one of her favorite quotes is:

"Injustice anywhere is a threat to justice everywhere. We are caught in an inescapable network of mutuality, tied in a single garment of destiny. Whatever affects one directly, affects all indirectly." **— Martin Luther King Jr., Letter from the Birmingham Jail**.